Giving Your Children Wings

Without Losing Yours

By

Tami Fox

Giving Your Children Wings

Without Losing Yours

Copyright © 2015 Tami Fox

Dedication

This book would not be possible without the love and support of my family: my husband, Jonathan, and our six children: Ashley, Nick, Jacob, Daniel, Quinton, and Ben. I especially want to thank Marla Cilley, the FlyLady. She supported me and encouraged me every step of the way in writing this book. I want to thank my prayer sisters: Tawdra, Tammy, Cindy, and Annie. You ladies have prayed me through a lot of tough times. I want to thank God for daily enabling me to do all that I do. I am blessed beyond measure.

This book is dedicated to my children and the beautiful blessings they have been to my life. God gave me the best children when He gave you to me. I pray that I raise each of you to be what God has for you.

Table of Contents

Introduction

God blessed me with six children. Raising them has been the greatest joy of my life. My family has inspired me to be the best that I can be. I was adopted as an infant, and I do not know my birth parents. My adoptive family is the family of my heart. My six children are the only people I know who are blood-related to me. It's a little strange to fill out medical information for myself and, at times, for my children because I do not have any family history. If you can believe it, some electronic medical record systems have no way of allowing for someone to have no family history.

My mother was married and divorced three times during my childhood, and my father lived outside of the United States for most of my childhood. My mother's third husband was abusive to her and to us, and it is just God's grace that I was able to forgive and move on with my life as an adult. I carry scars, but I don't carry bitterness in my heart. I know my mother and her parents did the best for me and my two younger brothers.

At different times in my life, I struggled with feeling abandoned, but I know that God will never abandon me. That gives me great comfort. I was raised in a multi-generational family with my grandparents, mom, and two younger brothers. My family tree looks a lot like a patchwork quilt that has been grafted with many branches. At various times, great-grandparents lived with us when I was growing up. So even though I do not have blood-line ancestry, I grew up in a loving family with lots of members. I never really knew how different my upbringing was from other people. I always thought my life was normal, and everyone lived with grandparents or close to grandparents. It was not until I was an adult that I realized not everyone was as blessed as I was with a large, extended family. I was raised going to church, and I went to private, Christian school for most of my growing up years. I went to public high school and graduated from there. I went to college and earned my Bachelor of Science degree.

My husband and I met through mutual friends, and we married two years after we met. We had our first child a year after we were married. At the time, we thought we wanted one or two children. God has a sense of humor, and we were blessed with one daughter and five sons. We were like most of our friends and family and sent our oldest child first to preschool and then on to public school. God worked on our hearts, and we eventually began our homeschool journey when our daughter was in 4th grade and our oldest son was in kindergarten. At the time, we also had a toddler, and I was pregnant with our fourth child. From the beginning, we knew we were doing the right thing for our family. I had always wanted to be a mom and a teacher, and when we started homeschooling, I got to be both. Frankly, I had always been their teacher, but now it was official with the state. When we started homeschooling, I felt like I got my children back from the system. I truly missed them when they were away at school. I am writing this book from the perspective of a homeschool mom, but I will include principles that will help moms with babies and preschoolers at home, homeschool moms, moms with children in school, and moms whose children have moved out.

Our early years of homeschooling were filled with lots of activities and family building time. There is a transition that occurs when you switch from traditional schooling to homeschooling. We had to learn how to work together as a team. I was drawn to hands-on learning since I had so many children. I found that I could combine subjects such as Bible, history, and science for everyone to study and do activities together. That freed up a lot of my grading and planning time. Each child was taught according to ability for language arts and math. I learned the strengths and weaknesses of my children. I learned new ways to teach the same concepts. By teaching with a hands-on approach, my children also learned quickly and remembered what they learned.

I do not teach to the test. I teach for mastery and for the love of learning. Homeschooling is as much of a learning experience for the teacher as it is for the students. In the past 15 years, I have learned so much more than I ever learned when I was a student. I was able to ignite a love for learning in my children and in myself. They know how to find the answers to their questions. I now have two young adult children, and both of them are glad they were homeschooled.

They feel that it benefitted them to learn at home. In high school, I made an effort to let them have educational experiences that would prepare them for adulthood. We talked a lot about careers and what they liked to do. My daughter said she was well prepared for college, and my oldest son completed an apprenticeship as a plumber. I strive each day to give my children a life full of joy and family.

Many people have asked me over the years what I do about learning gaps in my children. Let's be honest. We all have learning gaps no matter how we were educated. I chose to not let learning gaps stress me out. I taught my children how to find out information they do not know, and I prayed that God would give me what I needed to teach them according to His plan for their lives. There is great peace in that for me. I expose them to a variety of educational experiences, and I help them learn about things they are interested in. I also introduce new concepts to them and show excitement about what they are learning.

There have been hard years in our homeschool experience. Mainly, these were hard times within our extended family more than they were hard years educationally. We have had several significant losses in our extended family. In several of these situations, I was a caregiver for the family member. Providing end-of-life care for family is emotionally exhausting. My children learned a lot of compassion and empathy through these situations. They were not a part of the actual caregiving, but they visited the dying family members almost every day. We lost two grandparents within a six-month time period during one school year. I do not know how we would have been able to go through that time if the children were away at school all day long. We were there for each other. What I found is that living life is educational, so it is all linked. I had to learn how to walk through these valleys with my children, and I will say that I think we have better dealt with our grief because we homeschool and are together so much. I call these our heart lessons.

Having been through a lot of changes in my childhood from being adopted to parents divorcing, you would think that I would be bitter or have feelings of abandonment. I do not. I have spent a lot of time praying and reading the Bible over the years. I have some very wise friends who have walked with me through many years. I worked through my negative feelings, and I have forgiven those who hurt me in my past. In many cases, these people did not ask for forgiveness. I just had to do it on my own. That is a legacy I want to pass on to my children. I don't want them to hold on to pain and bitterness. As parents we make mistakes with our children. It is important to own up to these mistakes and apologize to our children. Don't dwell on mistakes. Live your life with purpose and peace. Let go of the bad feelings and negative thoughts.

My house has not always been neat and tidy, and I didn't always have a menu plan, but we always had an abundance of love. What I found is that I can raise my children, and we learned a lot together. Instead of losing parts of myself, I am giving my children the skills they need as adults. I am giving them their wings to fly. My children are now 24 down to 8. I have raised two children who are young adults and love what they do.

With praise and practice, I have shared some routines with my children that keeps our home tidy. I am seeing fruit from this in the homes of my young adult children. I learned most of our routines from The FlyLady (www.FlyLady.net). You will see her name often in this book.

Every day with my family is a gift from God. I work from home and write, but I always take time with my children each day to talk about what is important to them. I don't just have educational time with them, but I also spend time talking to them about the things that interest them. Now that my two adult children no longer live at home, I make an extra effort to talk to them or text them something encouraging each day. When they have problems or questions, they still come to me for advice.

As parents, we make mistakes with our children. It is important to own up to these mistakes and apologize to our children. Don't dwell on mistakes. Live your life with purpose and peace. Let go of the bad feelings and negative thoughts.

My purpose in writing this book is to encourage you along the way as you live life, raise your children, homeschool, and take care of yourself, your home, and your family. I have found some effective ways to make my home life more peaceful and easy to manage with routines set in place and good attitudes brought about by hard work and rewards. I want you to know that you can raise your children to go into adulthood and find their joy in life.

OUR GOAL IS TO RAISE CHILDREN WHO LOVE THE LORD AND SEEK TO FOLLOW HIS WILL FOR THEIR LIVES.

FOX FAMILY MISSION STATEMENT

Chapter 1

You Can Have a Clean House

Establishing routines in your home will not come together in a day or happen overnight. It will take patience, persistence, team work, and small steps. Habits do not just happen. Practicing routines every day will eventually lead to forming a habit. As you are learning new habits, include your children. They will benefit from establishing routines, too.

Endurance is the word I picked as my word for the year. If you wish to establish habits, endurance is a good character trait to have. It is not easy changing habits and routines. You might have to endure some tough feelings because establishing habits is very much a mental rewiring that you are doing over time to bring peace and order to your life and to your home. Stick with it. You will let go of the negative thoughts and embrace the positive as you establish new habits.

You might have seen a graphic of that claims that you cannot have a clean house and homeschool. I want to tell you that you can have a clean house and homeschool, too! If you are living with a lot of clutter

1

and are afraid to have people come inside your house, you need to commit to make changes to get rid of the clutter. You will need some routines. With a team approach, many hands will lighten your load. You can do it!

If you have not "met" The FlyLady (www.FlyLady.net) online, you need to visit her website and sign up for her emails to help you establish daily, weekly, and monthly routines. She also has control journals for adults and children that will help you with your routines. She has a Homeschool Teacher Control Journal, and she has a Student Control journal for you to give to your children to help them establish routines. You will baby step your way to a blessed home and a blessed life for your family.

Being a mom is a full-time job. Being a homeschool mom adds more to an already busy schedule. You have committed your time and your resources to educate your children at home. Keeping house in the manner that most of us learned from our mothers or grandmothers had a common thread of "do it right the first time or don't do it at all." When you buy into this perfectionism, you will find every excuse in the book to procrastinate taking care of your home. If you change your thinking and begin to work in small pockets of time, taking baby steps to declutter, and blessing your home with regular routines, you will find freedom from the chains of procrastination and perfectionism.

The biggest asset you have in blessing your home is teaching your children to love their home and bless it with you. I have raised, educated, and graduated two of our six children from our homeschool. Both of them are currently working full-time and running their own homes. Each of them has thanked me for teaching them how to care for a home and helping them to be prepared for adulthood.

Part of our homeschool is for everyone to learn how to prepare a complete meal, from menu planning to grocery shopping to preparing and serving the meal and cleaning up. We have participated in 4-H bake-offs and won prizes for baking cookies, breads, pies, cookies, and candies. We have worked together and learned to preserve food through canning and dehydrating. We have learned how to prepare a menu and shop the weekly specials. These are skills that I see paying off greatly in my older children. I involve my children in the whole process of cooking, so they are ready to do it on their own as adults. I do not do it in order for them to replace me and become my servants. I use the team approach as much as possible. We are all parts of the family unit, and we all work together for a common goal: a blessed home.

Your perspective sets the tone for your home. If you have a positive perspective on life and the obstacles you face in life, you will be a much happier person. This means your husband will have a happier wife, and your children will have a happier mother. We have all heard the saying, "If Mama ain't happy, no one is happy." You can turn this around to, "If Mama is happy, everyone around her is happy, too." A positive mood is contagious.

Do you view home keeping as a chore and drudgery? Is it something you have to endure? Is it something you ignore? Any of these perspectives will hold you back from receiving the blessings that come from having a clean and orderly home. Look at keeping order in your home as a blessing to you and to your family. Change a negative perspective and look for ways you can bless your family with a clean home.

Your children can be a part of this blessing. If you share with them the fun and joy you get from your home blessings, then it is something they will carry for the rest of their lives. By the same token, a negative attitude toward keeping your home will also go with them for the rest of their lives. Do not give children "chores" to do around the house as punishment. This will give them a negative outlook on their home for the rest of their lives. Find more positive words to use, such as tasks or routines.

A natural result of the amount of time we spend at home is that we work together to bless our home and keep it orderly. I start including them from young ages to help around the house. A two-year-old can fold washcloths and pick up things, especially toys they got out to play with. Teaching children in small steps to clean up behind themselves is a habit that they will carry with them. You want to do it in a positive way so they carry a positive attitude with them, too.

You have to let go of your perfectionism and let children learn; but, in the end, they can learn alongside you if you include them in everything you do. My goal has always been to raise my children to be independent, productive adults. I want them to achieve their dreams, and I give lots of opportunity for them to learn, make mistakes, make messes, clean up the messes, and grow.

Folding clothes can be a great time of fellowship and talking. It can even be a game. Lose your thoughts on perfectionism. Look at the effort and progress instead. A stack of washcloths folded by your young child may not look like a stack you folded; but in the end, does it matter if the stack is pretty? Brag on your little ones for helping you. Allow them to help you sort clothes and move them from washer to dryer. There are lots of ways even young children can help you with laundry.

Nagging children does not work. You need to use a different approach to teach your children to take care of their rooms and their home. The Student Control Journal from The FlyLady is a huge help in helping children gain control of the clutter and chaos in their rooms. The side benefit is that it is coming from The FlyLady's voice, and it helps take some of the pressure off you. The Student Control Journal is easily customized to fit your child's needed routines. She will help your child develop morning, afternoon, and before bed routines. Your child will learn about using a calendar and having a launch pad to put things together for the next day. The Control Journal will help your child develop zone cleaning routines for his or her bedroom. Later in life, your child will be able to use these same principles in caring for his or her home.

Life lessons are so valuable. I teach my children to take responsibility for their mistakes. We are all human, and we all mistakes. It's hard to watch your children make mistakes. It's easy to jump in and save them, but they really need to learn from their mistakes. Some of the hardest adults to deal with in life are those who were never taught to take responsibility for mistakes. A right attitude and forgiving spirit are parts of taking responsibility for mistakes. I give them school assignments that develop critical thinking skills; and, in the process, they do a lot of learning about how things work. Sometimes they learn how things don't work, and they have to solve the problem to make it work.

During the summer months, I spend time working and playing with my children. We work on learning new skills around the house, and we reward the hard work with fun activities. If children (and adults) know there is a reward in the end, it makes working much easier. When I am teaching my children something new, we work together. This helps me show them how to do something, and it also gives them a chance to come up with different ideas on how to do the task. Believe me, boys can find more efficient ways to do a task. I break my house down into different zones, and we focus on a different zone each week of the month. (See Appendix N.)

On week 1 of each month we focus on the living room and entry way. This is the second most-used room in our home, and it is very prone to clutter. While we do quick decluttering in the living room on a regular basis, we also need to spend some time focusing on the living room and what is in it. Does sitting in the living room in the evening evoke relaxation or the feeling of chaos? If it is the latter, you might need to spend more than a week decluttering and moving things around to make it peaceful. A home should be a place of refuge and relaxation. Look at what you have in your living room, and see if there are things that are not really necessary.

From the many years I have had with young children in the house, I do not have a coffee table in my living room. This keeps us from piling papers and magazines on a table in the living room. We do have side tables, so we have to be careful not to clutter these tables. It is just human nature to want things you like close to you. As I have worked alongside my children in the living room, I have let go of a lot of decorative items sitting around on tables, on the fireplace mantle, or on the bookshelves. Lots of little things sitting around mean more things to dust around. Rather than worry about them breaking something, I just display a few items that have meaning for us. There are lots of ways to simplify. Really look around your living room and decide if there are things that you don't really need in there. You can also spend fifteen minutes a day decluttering the front porch and dining room in the first week of each month.

After doing small, daily projects blessing our living room and entry way in week 1, we will move on to the next zone in week 2~the kitchen. The kitchen is the most-used room in my house. It is the heart of my home. We eat our meals and do school work in our kitchen. If we all pitch in together, we can keep the messes to a minimum, and it is not a burden on one person to keep it clean. With six people in the house, working in the kitchen can quickly become a burden on one person. Each person over the age of six can rinse his or her dishes and put them in the dishwasher. Dishes do not have to be piled in the sink for someone else to do later. The table and kitchen counters can be cleared and wiped down as they are used. The floor can be quickly swept up after a meal. After a family meal, we divide and conquer the work. One person clears the table. Another person rinses the dishes. Someone else puts away the refrigerator items. The fourth person sweeps the floor, and before you know it, the kitchen is back in order. It can be a time of fun and fellowship. We talk, laugh, sing, and enjoy working as a team. This time is an extension of our time together as a family.

Part of our zone time in the kitchen can also be routine maintenance that needs to be done. Doors and shelves need to be wiped off. Hinges and drawer slides may need tightening. What children don't love the opportunity to use tools to help fix something? Cabinets and drawers need decluttering, too. Making these routine projects fun for you and your children are blessings to your family. It is not just one more thing to do. View it as an opportunity to bless your family. Don't spend mega-hours doing these projects; use your timer. A quick 15-minute declutter project really adds up over time. When you are finished, find a fun activity that you enjoy doing together. My children know if we set the timer for a project that, when the timer goes off, we will do something fun. It can be as simple as going for a walk outside or playing a quick game of basketball in the driveway or playing a game inside. It can be as easy or involved as you like.

In the third week of the month, we focus on Zone 3-the bedrooms and bathrooms. We have four bedrooms and three bathrooms. We divide into teams in week 3 to do zone work in the bedrooms. We spend fifteen minutes each morning this week decluttering and straightening up. It is not a huge chore since we work daily on picking up behind ourselves. Twice a year we sort through the children's clothes and change over for the new season. This is also when we discard clothes that are worn out or too small. We also spend five minutes a day decluttering the bathrooms. This is a great time to get new toothbrushes for everyone and clean out drawers and cabinets. We do a quick swish and swipe in all of the bathrooms daily, so the bathrooms do not need a lot of deep cleaning.

The fourth week of the month brings us to zone 4. This is the week that we declutter and do routine maintenance in the laundry room and home office. This is my chance to clean the exhaust pipe from the dryer and hit the dust bunnies behind the dryer. I also use this week for end of the month paperwork in my home office. I sort mail and destroy junk mail daily, and I file bills as they arrive. The end of the month is the time to file paid receipts for my home office and shred the papers I do not need. The fourth week of the month is also when we change out air filters and check batteries. My children especially like working on little projects this week. It gives them the chance to shine in doing things that are helpful for the overall running of the home.

If the month has five weeks, I use this week as a maintenance week. We make a list of little things that need to be fixed throughout the month, so we have a list to check off. This is a great time to teach children how to fix things. We check doorknobs, handles on cabinets and doors, tighten screws where needed, check on things for safety, and more. We also check the living room, family room, or den area for any decluttering that needs to be done. We live and work in our home, so we need to maintain it and keep it in good working order. One day my children will grow up and have their own homes, and I want them to have good routines established now.

In all of our zone projects, we never spend hours and hours on projects. We use the timer and keep it short and sweet. Set your timer for 15 minutes and make it a game. This does not mean that you keep resetting the timer. Work for 15 minutes and STOP. Many hands make light work, and it is a lot more fun working as a team than as individuals.

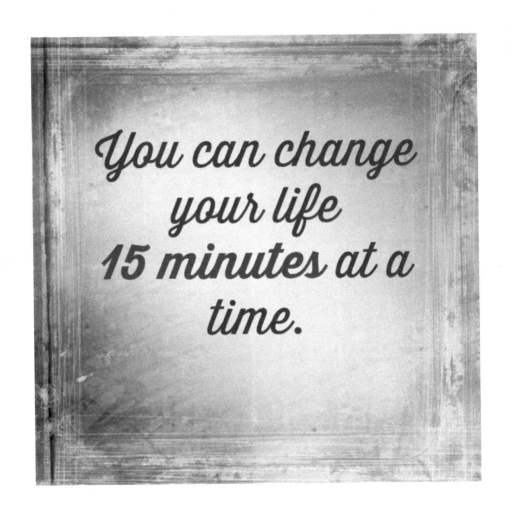

Chapter 2

Getting Rid of Clutter and Establishing Routines

Are you overwhelmed and living in CHAOS (Can't Have Anyone Over Syndrome)? When you homeschool, you naturally have additional stuff, such as educational materials and books, and messes seem to be made regularly, especially if you like to do crafts and hands-on activities. I have heard friends say that they can't homeschool, cook, and keep house all at once. Of course, you can't do it at once, but you can set up some routines, and you can do all three of these things daily. Routines will help keep CHAOS away.

How do you get a handle on all that stuff in your house?

Your house did not get cluttered and filled with stuff overnight, and it won't be decluttered and cleaned overnight. It will take small changes to your routine and a positive attitude daily to find your way out of CHAOS.

Several years ago, I stopped working outside of the home. Having come home to care for my children after working outside of the home, I had been used to working on projects with minimal interruptions. Suddenly, I was immersed in a life where I was interrupted frequently with the needs of my small children. I would start a task and very quickly became distracted. I was easily side-tracked. I needed to establish routines for myself and my family. Children thrive on a schedule. I started using The FlyLady system to declutter my home and set up routines. At this time my children were still young, but I included them in establishing our routines. If they were big enough to make a mess, they could help pick up behind themselves. I could not do it all.

When my house was in CHAOS, I tried to blame it on the fact that I had small children in the house. That was not the truth. The truth was that I did not have good routines established, and I had too much clutter in the house. I found out that I needed some set routines and a timer to help me tame the CHAOS. I had the kind of CHAOS that I really did not want my mother to come by my house unannounced; or, if she was coming over, I needed advance warning. (Are any of you in that boat?)

Getting out of CHAOS starts with a shiny sink. As silly as that might sound, as you walk through the kitchen and see your shiny sink, you want to do more to make your house match the sink. You want a whole, shiny house. By taking small steps in changing habits, you can tame the CHAOS and set some routines in your schedule. Your attitude about your home will spill over to your children. This morning, my son did the breakfast dishes and shined my sink without me asking him to do it. He was so proud of his job, and I praised him liberally.

Don't Go Anywhere on Monday

How do you like to start your school week off? I like to start it off on the right foot with my Weekly Home Blessing Hour, and that means I need to guard my Monday schedule. If at all possible, I do not go anywhere on Mondays. There are exceptions to this when I have to make appointments that just will not work on another day of the week. As a general rule, I will schedule appointments and field trips for any day of the week except for Monday. On the rare occasions when I have an appointment or field trip on a Monday, I feel like I am playing catch-up the rest of the week.

Another good reason to stay home on Mondays is to get the weekly menu plan in place and moving along. If possible, I will cook in bulk on Monday, and then I have easier meal prep and cooking the rest of the week. I make my menu plan and grocery list on Friday evenings. I grocery shop on Saturday. That way, I am ready to roll on Monday for our meals for the rest of the week. I don't know about your home, but in my home, everyone is happier if they are eating well and regularly. I use my slower cooker often. I love that I can turn it on to cook something at lunch time, and when it is time for our evening meal, I have something hot and ready. The best part is that it did not come from the drive-thru or pizza place. There are so many recipes for slow cookers these days, you can have quite a variety of meals using your slow cooker several times a week. If you keep salad fixings and vegetables on hand, you can put a well-balanced, healthy meal on the table every night.

My children have always been included in decluttering and house blessing. With a little music and enthusiasm, it can be fun to declutter. Children respond well to praise and rewards, and I always include rewards into our routines. No one wants to work all the time and not have fun, so I pick activities at home, outside, or away from the house as our rewards. One of our favorite rewards is to go fishing. Everyone knows the daily routine in our house, and they know if we get it done by 2:00, that we will have time to go fishing, weather permitting. This might not be an activity your children would enjoy, but you know what activity would spark the same enthusiasm for getting school work and routines finished early in the day.

We work as a team during the Weekly Home Blessing Hour. By dividing up the seven tasks, we are able to bless the whole house in an hour or less.

What are the Weekly Home Blessings?

Simply put, The FlyLady has a system developed for you to get your weekly house cleaning done in about seventy minutes on Monday morning (or evening). She has seven routines that will help you keep your home clean on a weekly basis without being a huge burden. If you have children in the home, you can include them in the Weekly Home Blessings and get finished even faster. I have gone through the times of having lots of young children in the house, and it is harder to include them in the home blessings, but stick with it and make it fun for them to help you. You are not looking for perfection here. You are just wanting to make a quick game of these seven routines.

You will want to have a timer handy and a quick list of these weekly routines. I have mine posted on the refrigerator, so it is easily seen by everyone in the family.

1) Vacuum

2) Dust

3) Quick Mop

4) Polish Mirrors and Doors

5) Purge Magazines

6) Change Sheets

7) Empty All Trash

Each of these seven areas can be handled differently when you are including your children. Some weeks, we take turns drawing from a hat to see which task we will do for ten minutes. Other times, we volunteer for what we want to do. Finally, there are just weeks when I assign each person to a task. I turn on some upbeat music, and we get busy. I have five boys who are easily distracted, so it helps that we are working in a very short time frame. It also helps that this is a weekly game for them, so we should not be buried in a lot of clutter and things that need to be moved around. By giving them clear directions, setting the timer, and playing music, they are successful with their tasks and don't lose focus. Since we are going to finish our home blessings in less than an hour each week, with four or five of us working at a time, it is not drudgery to do the weekly blessings. I will reward them at the end of the Home Blessing Hour in some way that makes them happy. I have found rewards are an excellent way to channel all the energy my boys have. Each task should take ten minutes or less. This is not the time to deep clean and move all the furniture. Deep cleaning and reorganizing will happen during Zone focus times throughout the month.

After we finish our Home Blessing Hour on Monday, we get our school week started off on the right foot. This is a really good reason for staying home on Monday. If we have a great start to our school week on Monday, then the rest of our week seems to flow much better. By doing this, I am not playing catch-up with their school work for the rest of the week. I also schedule our book work and reading pretty heavily on Mondays. This allows for flexibility later in the week if we need it. I set goals for how much school work I want accomplished each school year. Then I break it down into semester goals, monthly goals, and weekly goals. On Friday, I will sit down with these goals and create a lesson plan for each boy for each day of the next week. This way, I am able to see the big picture and track our progress. I can also work around vacations and field trips by having an idea of my goals for the year.

As the boys have grown, I have been able to slowly put more independent learning time into their schedules, but I know that many of you are homeschooling younger children who need a lot more one-on-one teaching with phonics and reading. Just remember that consistency and short lesson times when teaching reading can be a very good thing. Some of my hardest school years were when I was teaching reading to a younger child and teaching high school math and science to an older child. I got through those years by just taking it a day at a time and adjusting my lesson plans as needed. For the most part, we do our school bookwork 4 days a week. On the 5th day of the week, we have co-op, schedule appointments, or go on a field trip. So I assign two math lessons for each boy on Monday. That way, we still accomplish our 5 lessons for the week, and we are able to participate in outside activities. I use this approach with their other subjects as well. You can see where staying home on Monday to do our Weekly Home Blessing and extra bookwork makes the rest of our week flow better.

It takes focus, commitment, and a reward at the end to keep everyone motivated to participate in the Weekly Home Blessing Hour. Once the house has been blessed for the week, everyone is much more mindful to keep things in their places throughout the week. When they know that they will have to deal with their clutter over and over each week, they are much more motivated to pick up behind themselves the rest of the week. I schedule our Weekly Home Blessing Hour into my school day each Monday before we do our book work. This is real life learning, and it is only for one hour each week. They will take these skills with them into adulthood, and they will view it as a time each week to bless their homes rather than the drudgery of doing chores.

A big key to the Weekly Home Blessing Hour is to encourage children to do their best with a task, but not punish them or lecture them if they do not do the task to a perfectionist's standard. Do not get out the white gloves. Resist the urge to redo a task behind your children. The next week, rotate who does which tasks. This will help you see what each child does well. I have a friend who said she kept making her seventeen-year-old do the dinner dishes every night until he could get them done right. Her ten-year-old started doing the dishes over summer break, and she found that he did a better job with the dishes than his older brother. She wanted to keep making her older son do them until they met her specifications, but I encouraged her to let the younger son do them since he did a better job with them, and he enjoyed doing the dishes. Her older son can be given other tasks that he excels in and enjoys. Her older son understands the mechanics of doing dishes, and he can still help with them as needed.

Now, I hear you thinking in the back of your mind that I cannot possibly understand or know how your children are helping around your house. I have six children, and five of them are boys. Boys are not neat and tidy by nature, but they can help clean up the messes that they make. In our home, we do not divide tasks as boy chores or girl chores. We are all on the same team when it comes to routines and taming CHAOS. A two-year-old can help with routines. They will only be able to do simple things like picking up toys and putting them in a storage container. But if you model how to do it and make it fun, they will respond and help. As children get older, they can learn to help in more ways. If they are big enough to make a mess with their things, they are big enough to help clean up behind themselves. Mom or the older siblings cannot always clean up behind the youngest in the house. The way I approach the routines and Weekly Home Blessing Hour is that the youngest child does what he or she is capable of, and the more involved tasks go up the line to the appropriate person for the job.

If you don't have a lot of breakables around your house, you should be able to have a child do the dusting during the Weekly Home Blessing Hour. Another child can use a purple cloth with just plain water to wipe down windows, glass doors, or mirrors. You can give them one wet purple cloth and one dry purple cloth. This is a fast and effective way to get the windows cleaned without chemicals.

A child as young as eight or nine can sweep the floors. He or she can also use a mop to damp mop. You will have to be sure they know how much water to use if you have laminate flooring, but if you have tile or hardwood flooring, they can go to town on mopping. I have mostly laminate flooring or tile in our home, so we break it down into zones for the children to help me with the Weekly Home Blessing Hour in sweeping and mopping. I also monitor the amount of water they use on the laminate flooring during the mopping time because too much water on laminate flooring is not a good thing.

Young children can also be very helpful sweeping or vacuuming the staircase. They are just the right height to do the job, and it is a pretty easy job to do in our home. I include it in the time frame when we are doing the sweeping and the mopping. With many hands, our tasks can still be done in ten minutes, even with several rooms to do at one time.

If you have carpeting, your children can also help with the weekly vacuuming. Remember, you are not looking for someone to move furniture and vacuum underneath everything. You just want them to vacuum the middle part of the room and the areas that you walk on the most. You will get to the deeper Zone cleaning once a month where you hit the baseboards and under the sofa. You are not wanting to do a white glove treatment each week. You are blessing your home and your family.

Very young children can help you purge your magazines and paper clutter each week. Most of us have a place in our home that accumulates "stuff." The FlyLady calls this a Hot Spot. Your young children can help you clear the Hot Spot during your Weekly Home

Blessing Hour. Little ones love throwing stuff in the trash or into a container for recycling or donating. I try to donate magazines to nursing homes or leave them in doctor's offices. If you make a game out of it, they will think they are having the best time with you while you are getting your magazine and paper clutter under control.

This brings me to emptying trash cans. Small children love to go around the house with mom emptying trash cans. They think it is fun. Most moms don't think emptying trash cans is fun, but it can be fun. Fun can be contagious, especially if you are singing and dancing with them through the house. In our house, the kitchen trash is emptied daily, but we usually only empty the smaller trash cans in the bedrooms and bathrooms during our Weekly Home Blessing Hour. When a child is four or five, he or she can usually go through the house and pull out the small trash bags and bring them to mom for the big trash can. They should also be able to put a small liner or plastic grocery bag back into the smaller trash cans. I really recommend small trash can liners if you have young children helping you. That way, you have less chance of leaking happening along the way. (Personal experience talking here.) You also need to be aware of what is being thrown in your small trash cans because you don't want to expose young children to certain products. Since we do not use chemicals to clean, I don't typically have worries about what hazardous items might be thrown in our trash cans. We also have a rule that you don't throw items away with liquid in them. These few rules help keep the trash collection in the house from being messy.

Each week, bedding should be changed on all of the beds. If possible, you should have two sets of sheets for each bed in the house. During the Weekly Home Blessing Hour, you and the children can play beat-the-clock and strip all the bedding off the beds. You will have a pile of sheets and/or blankets for the wash, but next you are going to put on the clean, fresh sheets that you washed the week before. That way you are not waiting hours to re-make your bed. We have five beds to change each week, so it does take a little while to get all of the bedding washed, but I have found it helpful to have that second set of sheets handy to put right back on. One idea is to fold and store the extra set of sheets between your mattress and box springs, so they are handy when you pull the sheets off each week to wash them. You are not filling up a linen closet with extra sets of sheets by storing them this way.

If the weather is nice, it saves time and money to hang the sheets on the clothesline to dry. When the sheets are dry, they can be folded and put away for the next week's use. If you have young children who have accidents at night, you might be washing sheets more often, so you might already have two or three sets of sheets for the bed for the young ones in the house. I have found that during the potty-training phase, I do wash sheets more often, but I want to encourage you that the time will pass. You won't be washing sheets daily for the rest of your life.

Dirty Laundry Causes CHAOS in our Homes

Are you living with Mount Laundry in your home? I do not love doing laundry, and I am pretty sure many of you do not love it either. But I have decided to change my perspective on laundry. I do it daily because it blesses my family to have clean clothes. Many nights I am folding the last load of laundry just before I go to bed, and it is a time to reflect on my day and pray for my family as I do this last task of the day. I know they will be blessed to have clean clothes to put away when they get up in the morning. Sometimes I even fold the laundry for one of my older children when they have a load that finishes. It's just a simple task that takes a few minutes to do.

Many families live with piles of laundry. Some of it is clean, and some of it is dirty. Often, they are in the same pile. There are many methods that you can use to control Mount Laundry. The most effective method I have found is to do laundry daily. The next best thing you can do to tame Mount Laundry is to involve everyone from the age of two and up with the laundry. From age two, a child can help you move the laundry from the washer to the dryer. After the clothes are dry, a two-year-old can hand you one item at a time from the dryer while you talk and sing. As the child grows, you teach them different parts of the folding and putting away process. By the time a child is nine-years-old, he or she should be able to wash, dry, fold, or hang, and put away his or her own laundry, including bedding. Each child can be assigned a day of the week to do his or her laundry. You can move this task on your Weekly Home Blessing List. If you have a large family, you may have to assign two people per day of the week. We have six people in our home currently, so it works well to have a day of the week assigned to each family member. Well, I do lump my laundry and my husband's laundry into the same day since I also do our bedding. But I think you understand the principle I am sharing with you.

There are exceptions to the laundry day for each person. If a child gets sick or has an accident, I will help them no matter what day of the week it is. If we go swimming, I will do a load of all of the wet swimsuits and towels. Each person is responsible to put away his or her swimsuit. I fold and store the pool towels in a pool bag. If a child misses a laundry day, he or she will have to work the load into the system on another person's laundry day or wait until the next week to do two weeks' worth of laundry. This might be a problem if you have decluttered closets and don't have two weeks' worth of clothes for each person. As my children start part-time jobs or full-time jobs, they are still expected to do their own laundry and bedding. I don't do it for them. I don't rescue them if they fail to plan ahead and get their laundry done. They are learning cause and effect this way. If they are working, I am more flexible with them on choosing a laundry day. One son had a job where he had to wear a uniform, and he only had one uniform. So we worked his uniform in with other laundry as needed for his work schedule.

Besides my laundry, my husband's laundry, and our bedding, I also wash and dry the towels and washcloths. The boys fold them and put them away. I normally have a load of towels every day since I have six people bathing every day. I am not a fan of wet towels hanging in the bathroom to dry and be reused several times before washing. I have five boys, and I like for them to use a clean towel to dry off after bathing. I don't think they should use the same washcloth and towel for several days in a row. That is a personal preference of mine. You might have a different thought process on towels and washcloths, and I respect that.

If you are really behind on laundry, you can always go to the laundromat and do it all at once. I do not recommend this method as the way to deal with your laundry on a regular basis, but I do understand that, for some of you, it might make the most sense to go do it all at one time. Once you get it all washed, dried, folded (or hung), and put away, make it your goal to do at least one load of laundry per day. Get a system in place before you fall behind again. As I am sitting here writing tonight, my dryer is humming along in the background. I was out all day, but I am still doing one load of laundry today. After bath time tonight, I will likely have a second load to put in, but it will just be towels and wash cloths.

If you have a laundry routine established, you have probably already discovered three secrets. One is that you have to do at least one load of laundry a day to stay ahead of the mountain. In a large family, you might have to do more than one load a day to stay ahead of the dirty laundry mountain. The second secret to keeping dirty laundry from taking over is to have your children wash their own clothes once they are old enough to do it. The third secret is that you have probably thinned down the amount of clothing each person in your house has. I find it is a lot easier to maintain closets and dressers for the children if they do not have more clothes than they can fit in their areas for clothes storage. I live in an area where we have a change in seasons, so we have cold weather clothes and warm weather clothes. I have an area to store off-season clothing, but I am ruthless in purging those clothes. I throw out anything that has holes or stains. Since we are usually passing clothes down through the boys, I also ask them if they like an item or not. If they don't like an item, I donate it. I do not hold onto too many outgrown clothes. I like to pass them on to others if we don't need them.

We have a lot of mercy and grace and team work with all of our tasks, and this seems to help make the routines go faster and be more fun. If you make doing tasks around the house a game with a reward at the end, you will find more motivated people helping you. I always have a rule about assigning tasks to my children. I never ask them to do something that I am not willing to do myself.

You need to start small when you are taming the CHAOS in your house. The first step is to have a shiny sink. It makes me very happy to wake up every morning to a shiny sink. It takes practice, and it is something you need to share with your family. You never know when you might have an emergency or might be sick. I have a FlyLady Control Journal that outlines my daily, weekly, and monthly routines. My family knew that I had these lists, but they did not know what a shiny sink meant to my mental outlook each morning. I had surgery one December, and I found out quickly that a shiny sink was not something my family knew was important to me. I had to communicate this to them without being able to talk. I had to share my Control Journal with them. My advice is to tell your family about your routines, include them in the routines in your home, and tell them how important it is to you to have a home that is CHAOS-free. Share your control journal with your family.

When you get started with your routines, you want to make progress and not try for perfection. We can never achieve perfection in this world. You will instill a completely different attitude to caring for your home in your children by staying away from perfectionism. Do not use chores as a punishment for children, and avoid the word chores with them. Change your thinking. When you clean and declutter your home, it is a blessing to you and your family. Start using the term "Home Blessing" when you are going about your routines. Having a clean and clutter-free home is a blessing.

When your children grow up and have their own homes, they will have a positive outlook on blessing their family with a clean and clutter-free home. Most of us stumble on two things when it comes to cleaning our homes—perfectionism and negative thoughts about chores. You can change that for your children starting today. When you refer to the things you are doing to bless your home, use the terms, "tasks" and "routines." Both of these terms are more positive than saying the word, "chores."

The FlyLady also gave me a couple of other principles to live by in order to keep down the clutter in my home. The first one is the golden rule of keeping clutter at bay. When you bring something new into the house, you need to get rid of something. If you have a lot of clutter in your home, you might need to get rid of two things for each one thing that you bring home. It is preferable to get rid of something before you bring something new into the house, but I know how most of you are about letting things go. Ahem. You need to let go of stuff. You can't take it with you. Your children do not want to go through your clutter and get rid of it once you are gone. So, always keep a box in your trunk with items to donate. When you bring something new into the house, put something in the donate box. Once a week, stop by the local resale store of your choice and donate your items. It is that easy. When you are doing laundry, throw away torn clothing. If you see something go through the laundry that no longer fits the owner, get rid of it. Children and adults will do just fine without a large closet of clothes to maintain. Don't be overcome with too many clothes because that will cause you too much laundry.

Another principle to live by is the 27 Fling Boogie. If you do a 27 Fling Boogie just once a week, you will clear your house of clutter. What is the 27 Fling Boogie? I am glad you asked. It is a quick way to rid your home of 27 things quickly. You can trash things, recycle things, or donate things. The key is to get these 27 things out of your house. You can start simply. Do the 27 Fling Boogie with your piles of papers. Do it with your stacks of books. Have your children do it in their rooms. Set the timer for fifteen minutes. Turn on some music. Boogie your way to a clutter-free home.

You might have different areas of clutter that needs to be tamed, but I tried to list the major hot spots for most people. Use these principles and set yourself free of clutter. I have been decluttering for many years, and I still declutter daily.

We have more peace and harmony when we have a clean house, a good school day, and dinner on the table. I challenge you to clear your Mondays of outside commitments for six months (or even three months) and observe the differences in your home.

THE THREE R'S
FOR THE
HOMESCHOOL
MOM

ROUTINES
REWARDS
REST

Chapter 3

One Small Step at a Time

You have probably asked yourself how one small change at a time can really help you. Let's imagine a small snowball at the top of a hill. If you roll it down the hill, it will pick up more snow and get bigger and bigger. The same principle can be applied to making small, positive changes in your life. One small change can lead to another small change and on down the line until you have started the snowball effect.

In Chapter 2, you read about being overwhelmed and living in CHAOS. Have you started making changes and establishing routines that will help keep CHAOS away? Implementing small changes to your routines have a better chance of sticking than if you decide to make big, radical changes all at once. It all starts with a shiny sink, and it will spread to the rest of your house and your life.

Your house did not get this way overnight, and it won't be decluttered and cleaned overnight. It will take small changes to your routine and a positive attitude daily to find your way out of CHAOS. That is why you start with the shiny sink. It is a small area to start you off to taming the CHAOS in your home.

Besides the daily and weekly routines, you can also establish small, monthly routines that will help you transform your home from cluttered to peaceful and uncluttered. If you need a refresher on the Weekly Home Blessing Hour, we talked about it in chapter 2.

Monthly Habits

You need to start small when you are taming the CHAOS in your house. The FlyLady has a set of baby steps to help you get started. One of the Monthly Habits is Shining Your Sink. You are not behind if you haven't started doing it. Just start with Shining Your Sink today. Once you have the sink routine in place, you can start working on the current month's habit.

When you get started with your habits, you want to make progress but you don't need to be perfect. Because you will rotate through various habits over the course of each week and each month, you will be able to see the progress over time. One day, you will look back and realize that a much smaller amount of effort will need to be exerted to maintain a decluttered home. The best compliment I have received was from my eleven-year-old son. After reading the Monthly Habits, he said, "Mom, you do all of these every day."

January: Shining Your Sink

Shine your sink daily, preferably every time you cook. Teach your children to take care of their dirty dishes and leave the sink shiny after they eat. Make this a part of your bedtime routine, so you get up to a shiny sink every morning. This one small thing will set your day off on the right foot and make you smile when you walk into your kitchen. Now, if you are sitting there looking at a sink full of dirty dishes, take the hardest step now. Get up and go to the sink. Wash the dishes. Rinse your sink. Get a dry towel and dry it down. Now, look, you have a shiny sink. Let this one small thing become a habit. One day, you will see that this first step led you on the path to a clean and orderly home.

February: Declutter for 15 Minutes a Day

We all have stuff in our houses. Too much stuff. If you spend 15 minutes a day for 30 days decluttering, you will make a dent in cleaning out the extra stuff in your house. After you practice this habit for 30 days, you will find that you will declutter more often. The FlyLady Facebook page and emails will remind you to declutter at least once a day with a "Fifteen-Minute Hot Spot Declutter." This is simply taking 15 minutes to clear off the flat surface in your house that gets stacked on regularly. At least once a week, you can do a "27 Fling Boogie." It is as fun as it sounds. For 15 minutes, you pop in some upbeat music and throw out or put 27 items in a box for donations. After you finish your Flinging, you will take the trash out or put the donation box in your vehicle. That will get it out of the house. Do not bring anything back into the house from the donation box.

March: Getting Dressed to the Shoes

Getting dressed down to your shoes each morning is a habit that many people resist. If you get dressed all the way down to your shoes, you will be ready for anything the day brings you. I feel like a professional when I am dressed and have shoes on. I am not talking about wearing slip-on shoes, house shoes, or flip-flops. I am talking about lace-up shoes that do not come off easily. Wearing lace-up shoes will make you more productive. If you are concerned about germs and tracking in dirt from your shoes, you can always have a designated pair of lace-up shoes for the house. I have several pairs of lace-up shoes, and I rotate them for good foot health. This is a very easy and healthy habit to start. I have talked to several people about this one habit, and it is possible to live in the country with boys in the house and not have dirt and mud tracked in the house all day because they kept their shoes on. It comes down to training them. I train them from young ages to stomp the dirt and mud off their shoes outside. If they have particularly dirty shoes, they can rinse their shoes off with the garden hose. If they are doing barn chores, they can wear different shoes for animal care chores. The barn shoes get changed in the garage before they come into the house. My youngest boy is eight years old. I recently trained him to clean his shoes by showing him how to clean his shoes off outside. When he forgot, I would ask him to sweep up the mud and the dirt he tracked in the house. I stayed consistent and, within a week, he always remembered to clean his shoes off before coming in the house.

April: Making Your Bed

Do you make your bed every morning when you get up? Besides a shiny sink, having my bed made every morning sets the tone for my day. I am much happier when I walk in my room and my bed is made. It takes seconds to make a bed. I have a comforter, and I just pull it up and straighten my pillows. Then I do the same thing on my husband's side of the bed if he is already up for the day. He has grown so accustomed to seeing our bed made that he will straighten his side of the bed if he gets up after me in the mornings. It was not always like this, and I spent less time making the bed than whining about him not making the bed when he got up. Just do it. After you practice this habit for 30 days, you will not want to go back to having an unmade bed every day. I have also trained the boys to include making their beds as a part of their morning routine.

May: Let's Get Moving

May is a great time to get moving on your exercise. In most parts of the country, the weather is very pleasant in May. Flowers are blooming. Birds are chirping. Your body is ready for some vitamin D from the sun, so make a plan to move at least 15 minutes a day, preferably outside. Take your children outside and play with them. Go on a nature walk. Get your bikes out and go for a ride. There are so many things you can do to get moving and exercise your body. After 30 days of practicing this habit, you might find that you look forward to this time every day. I am outside 15 minutes a day at a minimum, no matter what the weather is. This is a time for me to recharge physically and mentally. This is also a time for me to model healthy behavior for my children.

June: Drinking Water

The typical American diet does not include enough water. Our bodies are made up of more than 50% water. Most women need a little more than 2 liters of water per day (http://www.mayoclinic.org/healthy-living/nutrition-and-healthy-eating/in-depth/water/art-20044256). Your actual need will depend on your age, weight, activity level, and time of the year. During the hot summer, you will naturally need more water each day to replace water lost through perspiration. Because I am a runner, my need for water is higher than someone with a lower activity level. If you don't like plain water, add some fresh-squeezed lemon, lime, or orange to it. Don't count drinking coffee or soft drinks as a part of your daily water intake. Caffeine in coffee or soft drinks actually depletes your store of water and can lead to dehydration. I use a refillable water bottle to keep my water cool and fresh. I refill it throughout the day and take it wherever I go. I have trained my boys very well on always drinking water and taking it with them. They know to take a bottle of water with them when we leave the house to do errands. As a general rule on how much water to drink each day, I try to drink the number of ounces that is equal to half of my body weight. (Basically, I try to drink 75 oz. of water a day.) Do the same thing for your children and encourage them to drink water daily. Don't rely on juices and sodas as an adult, and don't let your children either. Your health will be much better with more water and less sugary drinks. Your budget will also be helped if you aren't buying a lot of sugary drinks and juices.

July: Swish and Swipe

Is your bathroom clean? Would you be embarrassed to let someone use your bathroom? For some reason, bathrooms often are neglected and not cleaned until you need a scraper to clean the toilet and tub. There is a better way. A daily swish and swipe in the bathroom will take you less than two minutes, and the reward is a clean bathroom that you would not mind letting your mother use. Once I was in the habit of doing a morning swish of my toilet and swipe of my tub and sink area, I just don't think about not doing it. My routine is to take a morning shower and do my swish and swipe immediately afterwards. Even on days when I am busy, I make time to spend just a few minutes swishing and swiping. The boys take turns doing a daily swish and swipe in their bathroom. With four boys using one bathroom, it needs a daily swish and swipe. If you have boys in the house, you know exactly what I mean. I can say that the daily swish and swipe makes keeping the bathroom clean a very easy task. I was out of town for a week, and there were still people at home taking care of things while I was gone. When I got back, I had to do a deep cleaning of my shower, toilet, and sink area. I would much rather spend less than two minutes a day doing swish and swipe versus thirty minutes once a week.

August: Laundry

Does Mount Washmore reside in your house? Do you have a routine for doing your laundry? With a large family, I have had to establish a really good routine for our laundry. The FlyLady has a great saying, "A load a day, keeps the chaos away." If you are looking at a mountain of dirty laundry, you might have to take it to the laundromat and get caught up at one time. Then, you need to start doing at least one load of laundry a day from start to finish. What is start to finish? You need to wash, dry, fold or hang, and put away each load of laundry daily. In my house, we do more than one load of laundry per day. Monday is the day we wash our bedding. By having a designated day for washing our bedding, it is easier to do it weekly. Of course, sickness can change that; but, for the most part, our bedding is washed on Monday each week.

September: Before Bed Routine

Do you have a routine that you do each night before bed? This one habit can set the tone for how well your morning will start off the next day. By taking the time to lay out clothes, check your calendar, put out anything you need to have handy for the next morning, make sure your keys are where you can find them, clear a hot spot, shine your sink, brush your teeth, wash your face, and go to bed at a decent hour, your morning will start off on the right foot. No more getting up and stressing yourself and your family out when you are trying to get out of the house. My children also have a modified version of my before bed routine. We have a central launch pad area to put items we need first thing in the morning. I keep our calendar on the refrigerator, so it is easy for everyone to check for activities the next day.

October: Get Rid of Paper Clutter

Are you drowning in paperwork even in the digital age? Don't be a paper hoarder. Learn to keep the papers you need and toss the rest. Even if you do a lot of projects that involve cutting pictures out of magazines, you can still thin out your magazine collection each Monday during the Weekly Home Blessing Hour. You can donate magazines to a variety of organizations. Nursing homes and doctor's offices are usually good places to donate magazines. Keep a box in your trunk and toss in magazines once a week. When you are out doing your errands, you can drop them off at the place of your choosing. Don't hold on to junk mail. Purge junk mail daily when it comes in the mail. Have a designated place for filing bills, and set up your tax return files when you are doing your taxes. Each month, you can file receipts in your tax files. When it is time to do your taxes, your files will be ready for review. Don't hold on to your child's school paperwork in bulk. Keep the most important papers and share their projects with family members. You can take pictures of them with their projects for memory books. My adult daughter told me that her projects had more sentimental value to me than they had to her. If you still subscribe to a printed newspaper, consider donating previous editions to a local animal shelter. They use newspapers to line the floor for the animals in many cases.

November: Menu Planning

Does the thought of menu planning make you freeze in your tracks? Menu planning does not have to be complicated or extravagant. If you have never done a menu plan, start with a current month calendar. Each day, write down what your family eats for breakfast, lunch, and dinner. This will give you a guide on meals that you are already serving your family. Make notes on the calendar if they really like or dislike a meal. After you have a guide for what your family ate for the past month, you can sit down once a week and make a menu plan. I find that I save money, time, and my stress level if I have a menu plan. I normally sit down on Friday night and make a menu plan and grocery list for the next week. My grocery shopping day varies from season to season. Sometimes I shop on Saturday; other times, I shop on Monday. You can also subscribe to online menu planning services, such as SavingDinner.com or BuildAMenu.com. My menus do change seasonally to take advantage of fresh fruits and vegetables. I cook more stews and soups in the winter. But I will say that I use my slow cooker year round. I even take it with me on vacation to make meals easy for me. (See Appendix K for some suggested meal options.)

December: Pamper Yourself

Do you pamper yourself on a regular basis? If you don't, you should start immediately. I am not saying you need regular, out-of-the-house, spa days, but those are nice if your budget allows. You are worth pampering and taking care of yourself. It is not selfish to take care of yourself. You need to find ways to take care of yourself to rejuvenate and recharge. Find something that makes you feel good about yourself, and work it into your schedule on a regular basis. I like getting my nails done, so I get them done each month. I enjoy reading and sewing, so I work those into my schedule weekly or even daily. Writing has always been a passion of mine, and it is something that helps me process what is going on in my life. I try to find time daily to do some writing. My boys will make coupons for me to get pampering from them. I work hard to fill their love tanks; and, in turn, they do things for me that I enjoy. My husband is also learning to speak my love language and do things for me that fill my love tank. Pampering yourself does not necessarily mean spending money on yourself. If you don't have a clue of what to do to pamper yourself, spend some time making a list of things you enjoy that make you feel special.

All of this may seem overwhelming if you try to do it all once. I don't recommend you try to implement all of these steps at once. Just do one small step at a time. Sign up for the FlyLady's emails if you haven't already done that. Work through the steps with her guiding you. She has a Lite Version of her emails to get you started your first thirty days. Jump in with those emails. Pick up the Monthly Habit if you are doing well with the Lite Version of the emails the first thirty days. After you finish the first thirty days, just take off flying with the Monthly Habit of the month. Remember that it took time to get where you are, and it will take time to get where you want to go. Patience with yourself is very important. You do not want to burnout doing too much at one time. Get the FlyLady's Control Journal and build your own Control Journal with her guidance. The best gift you can give your family is a calm, relaxed, CHAOS-free home. It all starts with a shiny sink.

Small steps lead to big changes.

Chapter 4

Benefits of Homeschooling

Some of you reading this may not be homeschoolers but bear with me. Even if you are not "officially" a homeschool that is registered with the state, you still teach your children things. Read on. You might find some applicable tips. I consider all parents home educators because education begins at home.

When you have a baby, you start from Day 1 teaching them and loving them. For many months, you are the primary caregiver for your child. You are also his/her first teacher. You start by talking to your baby in order to help them to develop communication skills. You teach your child to eat. You help your child learn a sleeping schedule. Eventually, you will teach your child to walk and use the potty. You probably don't consider yourself a homeschooler since that is just not a term normally applied to children under the age of five. But really, you are your child's first teacher. You love your child like no one else does. Even if your child goes to daycare or has another caregiver, you are still your child's primary teacher.

When children reach school age, according to local or state laws, you get a little more serious about the terminology regarding your child's formal education. You have choices for educating your child. My choice is to homeschool my children. My older children did go to public school for a time, and I can say that deciding to bring them home for their education was the right decision for our family. If you are trying to decide between public school, private school, or homeschool, I want to give you some of the benefits I have seen from teaching my children at home. If you are already homeschooling, read on for some encouragement. The National Home Education Research Institute has gathered information from many studies on the benefits of homeschooling. I recommend their website: www.nheri.org.

Many people have asked me over the years what I do about learning gaps in my children. Let's be honest. We all have learning gaps no matter how we were educated. I chose to not let learning gaps stress me out. I taught my children how to find out information they do not know, and I prayed that God would give me what I needed to teach them according to His plan for their lives. There is great peace in that for me. I expose them to a variety of educational experiences, and I help them learn about things they are interested in. I also introduce new concepts to them and show excitement about what they are learning.

There have been hard years in our homeschool experience. These were primarily hard times within our extended family instead of being hard years educationally. We have had several significant losses in our extended family. In several of these situations, I was a caregiver for the family member. Providing end-of-life care for family is emotionally exhausting. My children learned a lot of compassion and empathy through these situations. They were not a part of the actual caregiving, but they visited the dying family members almost every day. We lost two grandparents within a six-month time period during one school year. I do not know how we would have been able to go through that time if the children were away at school all day long. We were there for each other. What I found is that living life is educational, so it is all linked. I had to learn how to walk through these valleys with my children, and I will say that I think we have better dealt with our grief because we homeschool and are together so much. I call these our heart lessons. I decided that we had 365 days in a year, and if we had to do math lessons and reading over the summer, it was important that they have the time they could spend with their grandparents before they passed away. Even though these times were hard, I think the benefits of continuing to homeschool were worth it.

For school organization, I have a bookshelf and a cabinet in my kitchen, and it has closing doors for our books and supplies. Each child has a section in the cabinet for the current year's school books. I store craft supplies in the drawers of the cabinet, and I have a bookshelf nearby for current year resource books. I have tried various methods over the years to organize our school books, and this seems to work the best for us. We also attend a weekly co-op, and each child has a backpack for co-op.

Each child has a planner book for daily assignments. This serves as a check off for them and for me. I am really low tech for this. I like to use pencil and paper and have a page for each school week. By writing in pencil, I am able to make changes if we have unforeseen changes to our schedule due to sickness or whatever might throw us off schedule. I have tried other methods, but I found this gives my children a tangible check off sheet for each day, and it keeps me on track for meeting our educational goals. They also learn to keep track of their school work with a daily check-off sheet.

How I Plan My School Year

In the spring and summer, I spend time researching, praying, and planning our upcoming school year. I talk to my husband about goals for each of our children. This can include educational goals, spiritual goals, and life goals. I make book lists and check my resources on hand. Then I know what I need to buy or borrow.

Based on state requirements, I plan based on a nine-month school year as an overview, and then I take the actual books and divide them up according to the number of school days we have, which is 180 days in our state. This way I know how much to assign each child daily and weekly. I use pencil to make a weekly assignment plan with daily check offs for each of my boys. The reason I use pencil is because things happen to interrupt our schedule. Kids get sick. Appointments come up. Accidents happen. One fall, a small flood in the bathroom derailed four weeks of planned bookwork. I have had to learn mercy and grace and flexibility in our homeschool journey.

Setting Goals for Your Homeschool

When you are planning your school year, it is good to know what your family mission statement is. Our family mission statement and homeschool mission statement are the same. We want to raise children who love the Lord with all their hearts, minds, and souls. Everything we do is based on that.

My husband and I talk to each other about goals for our children, and then we talk to each child about the goals God has laid on our hearts for them. We also listen as they tell us what they feel God is preparing them for in life.

Each year we have three areas in which we set goals: spiritual goals, educational goals, and life goals. Their spiritual goals come from areas we see they need to focus on concerning character growth. Each child will usually have different spiritual goals based on age and maturity. But there are times when they all need to work on obedience or forgiveness. Educational goals are set based on their age and current progress in their schoolwork. We look for areas where they may need remediation, and we look at areas where they are excelling and may need to move on faster than I had planned. We also talk to them about life goals. If they have particular strengths or interests, we try to bring in activities that will enhance this. For some of our children this has been sports, music, or apprenticeships.

We know that we will have things we miss teaching our children along the way. Our prayer is that God will fill these gaps and help us to train our children for what He has for their lives. It is our belief that God will equip our children for what He calls them to do in adulthood. I know that I cannot possibly cover every single subject in the world. I know they will have some learning gaps. I don't stress about learning gaps. I teach my children how to research and read about a variety of topics, and I know they can research information from reputable sources by the time they graduate from our homeschool.

Schedule

My homeschool schedule is set by me. I have control of our schedule. It does not have control of me, and it does not come from an outside source, such as a public school or private school calendar. I can decide when to start our school year and what time of day we do our schoolwork. I don't worry about weather-related issues such as missing days for snow. I do allow for sick days in my school scheduling. I do not think a sick child should ever have to do school work. Our school schedule only has to have 180 school days per calendar year. I pick the 180 days, and there are years when we homeschool year-round and take breaks during the year to accommodate travel or other time off from school. (See Appendix J for a Sample School Schedule.)

How do I Stay on Task?

Staying on task is very hard to do when you are running a house and teaching school, too. I have some tips that have helped me over the years with staying on task with our school day. Using a timer is a key component for me to keep my focus on a task at hand. Training my children to return to their schoolwork after a short break is also a big key to staying on track. Children need breaks in between subjects, and with boys, they need to exert some large muscle energy. I encourage them to get outside and play for a few minutes in between subjects, but I have also trained them to come back inside to finish the rest of their subjects. This means I have to stay on task and not get distracted myself.

1. Schedule a time for school.

We do school in the mornings. There have been seasons when we have had a new baby in the house, and we did school during baby's naptimes or in the evening when my husband was home and could help with the baby and/or toddler. When I was on bed rest during pregnancy, I oversaw our school from my bed or the sofa. We worked in really short time periods throughout the day. The children learned a lot about reading and research during those times. But even if I changed the location or time of our school day, we still did school daily.

2. Limit outside distractions.

Let's face it, a lot of our well-meaning friends and family think because we are home we are free to talk on the phone or meet for lunch or go a fantastic ladies' Bible study anytime we want. The reality is that being a homeschool mom is a full-time responsibility. I have had to limit outside commitments during the weekdays in order to do the job I am called to do in my home. The years you spend homeschooling will only be for a short season. Before you know it, your children will be grown and through with their schooling at home. Don't over burden your schedule with lots of outside activities during the homeschool years.

3. Turn off your phone.

Many of us have phones that ring a lot. Some of us have smart phones that also bring us text messages, emails, and links to social media. During school time, turn off the phones. Let voice mail pick up your calls. Ignore the beeps and dings of your smart phone. Yes, emergencies happen. In my family, they seem to happen a lot. But I try to give my undivided attention to my children as much as I can during school time. I can check emails, text messages, and voice mails when they are doing independent work.

4. Close the computer.

Unless you are using the computer for a school lesson, close it or turn it off. It is very easy to get sucked into emails and social media on the computer. It is also easy to get off on a rabbit trail on the computer doing research for school work. (Ask me how I know this.) So close your computer and get school done with your kids. I promise the stuff on the computer will still be there later.

5. Limit appointments.

We all have outside appointments–co-ops, doctors' appointments, dentist appointments, supplemental classes, field trips, and on and on and on. There is not a problem finding things to do outside the home. But I encourage you to limit these outside appointments during your school day as much as possible. In this season of our homeschool, we participate in a weekly co-op. I am very careful with what I plan during the mornings the other four days of the week. I have learned over the years that if we have a morning doctor's appointment or dentist appointment, it is hard to come home and get everyone back on task with school. As my children have gotten older, it is easier to get back on task and complete our school day after an appointment, but for the years when I had lots of little ones in the house, if we had an outside appointment, we usually lost that school day's planned bookwork because we all needed a nap after a morning outing.

6. Let Your Children Move Around During the School Time.

Children need to move around during the school time. With training, they will get used to having a time to move around and get back on their planned work for the day. Please do not expect your children to sit from the time they start their lessons until they are finished for the day. They should get up at least once an hour to move around, get some water, and go to the bathroom. Children with a lot of energy can do some physical activity for five or ten minutes each hour and come back to their schoolwork with a renewed focus. This is a time for you to move around with them and refill your water bottle. I have active boys, and they do a better job with their lessons with time to move around each hour.

By working on these areas, I have found that it is easier to stay on task and complete our goals for school.

Choice of Materials

As a homeschool teacher, I get to pick out which books and educational opportunities I want for my children. I do not have to use items that don't fit the learning style of my children. Some of my children are visual, and some are auditory. One of them is a very highly kinesthetic (hands-on) learner. Because homeschooling is individualized for the student, it is more effective. I have also learned a lot alongside them. There are so many choices in books and materials for homeschooling that it is a little overwhelming to decide what works for your family. My best advice is for you to attend a homeschool conference and look at what is available. If you can't do that, do some research online, but you should also look for a local homeschool support group. Many groups will have question and answer nights for new homeschoolers or those considering homeschooling. Some groups will have a curriculum share night where moms will bring books for others to see in person.

No More Homework

If you have a child who has a lot of homework, this might be a huge thing for some of you. My children do an entire school day's work in the same amount of time some children do homework. For my children under high school age, our school day is usually finished at lunch time. There are some days when it stretches into the afternoon, but that is rare. My high school students spend more time on their school work than the younger students. Their day typically has a morning and afternoon session with a lunch break in the middle. I do not miss homework days from when my older two were in public school.

Better Family Relationships

The best benefit of homeschooling for my family has been seeing my children develop better relationships with each other, with my husband, with me, and with their grandparents and extended family. We have more time for family and special activities that interest us with our homeschool schedule. We can see extended family during the day or in the evenings. I love having our evenings free to spend together as a family. We have family dinner each evening, and during that time, we talk about what we learned today. This is a great review, and it communicates to my husband what we are leaning each day.

If you are considering homeschooling to shelter your children or think that it will prevent bad things from happening to your family, this is probably not the best of reasons to homeschool. Homeschool families still experience financial and health difficulties. Homeschool families are not untouched from divorce or abuse. Homeschool teenagers still go through phases where they make poor decisions and mistakes. Homeschooling is a lifestyle, and it can be a protected lifestyle in some ways, but it is not possible to have complete protection from the world. We live in a fallen world full of imperfect people, and no matter if you decide to homeschool or not, you will still have to deal with the ramifications of living in a fallen world.

Creative Learning

With both younger children and older children in the house, we have used creative ways to learn. Time spent cooking and baking can reinforce math and reading lessons. Following a recipe can help teach sequencing, fractions, and equivalent measurements. With a large family, we often double recipes. This is a great way to practice adding fractions. We also make grocery lists, clip coupons, and grocery shop to practice our math skills. We talk about budgeting and saving money while doing these activities.

We practice reading skills by reading labels on items, or reading road signs while riding down the road. We can play A-B-C games. I teach my older children to read road maps and learn North, South, East, and West on a compass. Even in a world with GPS, it is important to know how to read a map and navigate. There are times when a battery on a GPS dies, or there are times when you lose the signal on your GPS. In these instances, you will be glad someone can read a map and navigate for you while you are driving. I teach this skill to my children before they ever take a driver's training course.

Creative Lessons with Toddlers and Preschoolers

When planning school lessons for my older children, I always plan age-appropriate things for my youngest ones to do. I pick out picture books with similar themes to what my older children are learning about. This helps build family ties, and if I have a young reader in the house, I have them read out loud with the younger ones, too. I also have toys available for the younger ones to play with while I read chapter books to my older children. This strategy helps build a strong vocabulary in my young children. As my toddlers get closer to age three, I make lots of little games for them to play that incorporate numbers, letters, matching, and sequencing activities. All children learn as they play, and my goal is for them to develop a love for learning at a young age. I have found that my little ones absorb all of the oral communication that goes on during the day, and they often have been very easy to teach reading and math because they have heard so much reading in our home. They also have heard math facts being practiced daily, and they usually start kindergarten with a very good base in math and vocabulary.

Toddlers have a lot of energy, and I plan active learning games with them, too. We sort and play with stuffed animals and build with blocks and do lots of games that include movement. We play store or restaurant. I also plan activities and games for my older children to play with my younger children that is an extension of their schoolwork. This enhances their relationships with one another and builds family ties while they learn and play.

Preschoolers need to work on fine motor skills, so I provide lots of arts and craft materials once they are past the age where they put everything in their mouths. Here are some ideas:

- Finger paints
- Salt dough
- Water colors
- Glue/Paste
- Stickers
- Crayons
- Safety scissors
- Construction paper
- Old magazines
- Pipe cleaners
- Large beads and string
- Paint pens
- Washable markers
- Shaving cream art

- Pudding art
- String pasta

This is a just a list to get you going. You can come up with lots of ideas for manipulatives for young children to use.

Another way I have found to creatively include all ages in our learning adventures is to plan field trips. I pick field trips that go along with what we are studying and will give them a better understanding of what we are learning. They remember so many details from our field trips, and this is a great way to reinforce learning. Sometimes we go on the field trip before we study a subject, but more often we study something and then go on a field trip. Some of our field trips are dictated by season or by the schedule of the people responsible for the activity. I love hearing the different interpretations of what they have learned when we go on a field trip.

Music is a great way to include both younger and older children in learning times. Most history time periods have music that was written during it. I use the music in the background while they are working on arts and crafts projects or other quiet activities. We talk about the composers and time period very conversationally, and I have seen lots of information retained by my children when they were really young from this informal music time. It does not have to be elaborate. I have used music CDs from the library and YouTube videos for much of our music time. I don't spend a lot of money buying music when I can access so much for free through other resources. Music can enhance their memory of things learned.

We also play games and do little dramatizations with all ages. Young children enjoy playing dress up and acting out events. I read a Bible passage or historical event aloud, and then I let them work up a script and come up with costumes. This engages many parts of their brains and causes them to have vivid memories of these little dramas. I have had them recount memories from participating in a drama from as early as age three. It is astounding what they retain when they experience something versus just reading or listening to a story.

My toddlers and preschoolers are never made to feel that they are an interruption to our school time. They are included as much as possible in what we are doing. I have seen so many positive outcomes from this approach. It is possible to teach high schoolers while having little ones in the house. My oldest child was fifteen when I had my sixth child. Like the ones before him, he sat on my lap a lot as a baby while I taught lessons. As he grew, I adjusted our surroundings with the use of a pack-n-play in the kitchen and toys in the living room. I would rotate activity stations for the youngest one so he was never put off by my time of teaching with the older ones. I would save intense one-on-one teaching time for nap time, so the older children did not suffer in their learning either. A lot of my creative learning ideas were born out of necessity to balance teaching multiple ages. Some of our best learning memories are from the times when we had several little ones in the house. One neat benefit of having him around our lesson times is that he has been the easiest child to teach to read and memorize math facts. Little ones should never be viewed as a hindrance to the learning process for your older children.

1. Schedule a time for school
2. Limit outside distractions
3. Turn off the phone
4. Close the computer
5. Limit appointments
6. Encourage movement

Chapter 5

Taking Care of Yourself

As women, we go through different seasons of life. New moms are usually sleep deprived and run on empty all the time. New moms sleep with one ear open, and night-time sleep is often broken up by a hungry baby. For some, a new baby in the house may also have older siblings, which means mom is not getting a full night's sleep and also is not able to nap during the day. If you have a baby in the house and someone offers to help you, take them up on it. The first several months after you have a baby is a time when you need to find a way to rejuvenate and rest when possible. The side effects of long-term sleep deprivation is not a good thing. You don't have to be super mom.

Most moms are selfless. They put everyone else before themselves. It is a part of our nurturing side as a woman and caregiver. From experience I can tell you that always putting others before yourself and your health can be unhealthy. I had to decide that I loved myself enough to make some healthy changes in my life. I had to choose to exercise on a regular basis. I had to choose to eat healthy foods. I had to choose to put taking care of my spiritual needs back into the center of my life. When life gets crazy with changes, such as new babies, sick family members, or the death of family members, it is very easy to stop taking care of yourself. I want you to stop that thinking and remember that no one else can take care of those around you like YOU would do it. So you have to make it a priority to schedule time for self-care into your day.

If you are a homeschool mom with a new baby, you need to really scale back on how much schoolwork and activities you have scheduled for the first six months. You should also try to schedule time off from school right after the baby is born. I suggest anywhere from one month to three months depending on your recovery needs. I have six children, and I had four of them after we started homeschooling. I had them at various times of the year, so I always worked toward getting in as many school days as possible before the baby was born. I had high-risk pregnancies, and I was on bed rest. I learned to do school with the older children from my bed or sofa. As much as possible, I allowed myself three months after the baby was born before starting a full school schedule with the older children. Even then, I started back slowly with them doing as much independent work as possible before I went back to full-fledge teaching. I also used evening time when my husband was home to do one-on-one teaching, if needed, when we had a baby in the house. When I had our sixth child, I had a high school student to teach. I saved algebra teaching time for evenings because she needed my undivided attention for that subject even though she was using a computer program for the lessons.

With babies, toddlers, and homeschooling going on all at once, it is very easy to get to the point where you are running on empty. You need to talk to your husband about ways you can have some downtime and rest and refill your tank. Raising children is a marathon. You need to pace yourself and find times to relax. You can find these times in a lot of different ways. If your children are young, you can have an afternoon quiet time for everyone after lunch time. Each person, no matter what his or her age, can have quiet time for thirty minutes to an hour. Young children can nap, and older children can use this time to rest or read on their bed. I would suggest that you not allow older children to have electronics during quiet time, but you might find it handy to let them listen to audio CDs. This is a good time for them to get in some daily reading time. Quiet time allows mom to have a quick nap or just rest quietly. It might take some persistence in training the children to have this quiet time if you have not done it before, but it is worth it.

From birth, children take a lot of time and effort. I used to hear people talk about how it is hard raising children when they are young and need a lot of hands-on help. Their needs change as they get older, and often the emotions you put into raising and talking to your older children is just as draining as the physical care you gave them when they were younger. Older children and young adult children have different needs from younger children, but they still need you. What I love about homeschooling is the relationships I have with my children. My young adult children have full-time jobs and have moved out of our home. They both call and text me regularly because we have spent years talking and investing in communicating with one another.

Take time to enjoy your children and have fun with them while they are growing up. I work from home, and I am also a writer. I find ways to work in my writing time and work time without using the TV or computer games as a baby-sitter. Case in point: Today I needed to get a certain number of words written in this book. So I brought the boys to the river so they could do some fishing while I sit with my laptop and write. I stop every now and then to admire their catches and take pictures. Then, I sit back down to do some writing. They are getting their love tanks filled doing something they enjoy. I get to sit in my chair and do something I love. Finding ways to do things that I love to do helps keep me from running on empty.

Another strategy I have found to keep me from running on empty is to have date nights with my husband. This has been harder at times depending on the ages and number of children we have. But we make it a priority to go out on a date night as often as we can. We have been blessed with family who will watch the children for our date nights, so that helps the expense factor of date night tremendously. Even when our budget has been tight, we have found creative and inexpensive ways to have date night. It does not mean that we always go out for date night. We have had at-home date nights on occasion. I do like going out with my husband to get away from the distractions of the house, but there are times when it is just not possible to go out on the town for a date.

Spending time with the Lord is also a great way for me to beat the running-on-empty feeling. To keep my spiritual tank from running on empty, I spend time daily reading the Bible and praying. I also have a really good support system of friends who are my prayer partners. They have seen me through a lot of tough times.

Many of us will become caregivers to family members. Some of us will care for parents or grandparents. We may also become caregivers for a spouse or children. Studies have shown that caregivers often develop health concerns of their own. It is imperative that caregivers take care of themselves, too.

One of the hardest seasons where I knew I was running on empty every single day was when we did in-home health care for my husband's parents while homeschooling and raising six children. I was so busy meeting everyone else's needs, and I let myself get run down and in an unhealthy place. I had to learn to set boundaries and say "No" to just about everything that came my way. I could barely keep my head above the water of the demands around me. I had to learn that I was important, too, and I had to find time to re-charge my batteries. When opportunities came for me and my family to get away for the day or the weekend, I took it. I had to physically remove myself from the house to relax and re-charge. That sounds a little extreme, but it was an extreme situation that went on for more than a year. You may find yourself in a similar situation. Take my advice and carve out time for you. You are important. You matter. Your health matters. You can only push so far before your health will be affected. I am four years past that time in my life, and I am still dealing with some health issues that arose from the extreme stress I was under during those months. Being an unhealthy mom is not a good thing for you or your family.

Exercise

It might sound counter-productive to tell you to exercise to help you to keep from running on empty, but you need a regular time to exercise to build your strength, health, and endurance. Just walking for fifteen minutes a day can make a big impact on your health, both physically and mentally. I am not telling you to go out and spend hours a day exercising. I am just saying to start with 15 minutes a day. You can do this on your own, or you can do it as a family. I really like doing something active with my children every day. It can vary from walking to playing basketball in the driveway. We live out in the country, so we like walking outside in the woods often. It is a way to get some exercise and observe nature. It can be both science and PE all in one. Homeschooled children traditionally move around and get more exercise than their peers who are in school all day. This means they are usually healthier and not overweight. My doctor has mentioned this to me many times because none of my children are overweight. Being outside has a calming effect on me and my children, and it is a good way for all of us to de-stress. No matter what the weather, the children and I go outside every day for a run or a walk. My stress level and blood pressure are both lower thanks to this time I take time each day to take care of myself.

After spending several years caring for elderly family members and my own family, I developed an auto-immune disease and high blood pressure. I have spent the last two years taking care of my health first, and I am healing. I will have an auto-immune disease and deal with blood pressure issues for the rest of my life. When they say high blood pressure is a silent killer they are serious. If you are neglecting yourself and have high blood pressure, you need to seek medical help. By exercising, eating healthy, and taking prescribed medication, I am healthier now than I was two years ago. Putting myself first has made a difference in my health.

My health issues were compounded when I began to take care of my husband's dying mother. She had ALS, and it was devastating to me emotionally. When I was caring for my mother-in-law, I was professional and dealt with the situation. But after I would leave her house, I would fall apart emotionally. At the time, I was a full-time college student, home educator, and had six children in the home. My stress levels were very high, and I had very few outlets for relaxing and taking care of myself. I was either being productive with something or sleeping. There was not a lot of in between these two. It took many months, but the family finally agreed to have my mother-in-law placed in a hospice house. We were all struggling with the demands of her care. She was also not dealing well with the pain and emotions of dying. It was in her best interest to have outside care.

While she was in hospice house, my father-in-law passed away. After a short stay in the hospice house, the family decided to bring my mother-in-law back home. I made a stipulation that a nursing agency would be used for her care. The family's main role would be to visit and love on her, while the nursing staff provided care for her. It took two caregivers during the day and one caregiver at night to give her the level of care needed. She was in her home five months later when she passed away. During those five months, my role was to walk my children through this loss and the loss of their grandfather.

After my mother-in-law passed away, some of my children took the loss very hard. Some of them held a lot of emotions inside. I spent two years really focusing on the emotional needs of my family. I did not spend a lot of time working on my own emotional and physical needs. All told, I spent three years not taking good care of myself. I decided in early 2012, that it was time to start taking care of my health. By this point, I had several significant health risks, had gained weight, and had developed an auto-immune disease. I was living proof that caregivers can put their own health at risk by putting the needs of others ahead of themselves for a long period of time.

For most of my adult years I had exercised and had regular routines for getting in some time for strength training and cardio workouts. I had been derailed when providing end-of-life care for family members, while also having six children in the house. It was hard to get back on track. Over the years, I had mostly worked out at home. That seemed to work the best with small children to care for. I could do exercise DVDs early in the morning when they were sleeping, or they could even workout alongside of me. When the needs of dying family members became a daily need, my exercise routine fell to the wayside.

After the grieving process for me and my children, I decided one day that I was going to get back to my healthy exercise habits. But what did I want to do? I had a lot of stress and grief bottled up, and I needed to find a release. I decided to start running. I made a small goal of running a 5K, so I got an app for my phone called "Couch to 5K" (C25K). It was an inexpensive app, and it helped me start out with alternating walking and running. Each week, the app extended the amount of time that I would run versus the amount of time that I walked. I was overweight, out of shape, and asthmatic. I was not exactly a candidate for being a great runner. But I had determination. I slowly started out with running/walking three days a week. I learned to control my pace so I could breathe. I learned to push through the pain of working out muscles that had not been worked out in a long time. I learned that I was stronger than I thought.

Over time, I fell in love with running. It helped me reduce my stress. Running helped me lose weight. My blood pressure went down to the point that I was able take a smaller amount of my blood pressure medication. My children would run with me, so I was teaching them healthy habits through my example. I started running races and having goals for increasing my distance. To date I have completed races from a 5K to a full marathon (26.2 miles). I have completed mud runs, obstacle courses, and a triathlon. I run every single day, and I run outside most days. I just celebrated running 365 days in a row without missing a day. I have learned a lot about myself and how to dig deep to get through hard things.

I had to change my thinking and put my health back on the front burner. I mattered. I was important. I wanted to live long to see my children grow up. I wanted to see my future grandchildren.

Eating

Food choices can become a loaded topic for many women. What I have learned is that it is possible to plan, shop, and eat healthy on a budget. I have several strategies that have helped me along the way. I have read the *Trim Healthy Mama* book, and I use principles from it to guide me in my menu planning. I also use an online subscription service called Build-A-Menu (www.BuildAMenu.com). Build-A-Menu helps with menu planning and budgeting. It also helps save time by generating a shopping list based on my store of choice. I have also used Leann Ely's www.SavingDinner.com site to help me with meal planning. Leann also has several books designed to help you plan menus and cook meals that your family will enjoy. One of my favorite books of Leann's is her low-carb cookbook. It is important to sit down and eat as a family many times per week to build relationships.

It is much easier to eat healthy when I have a menu plan and shopping list every week. I strive to provide healthy, economical meals that feed a large family. I make time in my schedule to sit down and make a menu plan for breakfast, lunch, and dinner for the coming week. I consult my calendar and check with my husband for any special requests. I also look at our school plans to see if I can incorporate a cultural meal into our weekly plan. I check my cabinets and freezer to see what I have on hand to use for meals. Then I just start filling in boxes on a spreadsheet with items I want to cook. Build-A-Menu is designed so that you pick recipes, and it builds your menu and shopping list all at once.

My children participate in the planning and cooking process as much as possible. This helps them become an asset in the kitchen for me now, and it will benefit them later in life. Boys can cook as well as girls, and sometimes boys are better cooks than girls. If you think about well-known chefs, you might notice that many of them are men. Children also tend to eat a larger variety of foods when they are a part of the process in deciding what to eat and in preparing the food. I encourage my older children to create menu plans, shopping lists, and take a night of cooking as the head chef. I don't mind being a sous-chef to help my children gain experience and confidence in the kitchen.

The best secret weapon in meal preparation is my slow cooker. I regularly plan meals that I can start in the slow cooker at lunch time and, by dinner time, I have a hot meal ready. I just need to pull out the salad ingredients, and we have dinner ready without me spending hours in the kitchen. Crock pot meals can be tasty, healthy, and economical. If you are not using a crock pot regularly, get one and start using it.

What I realized is that everyone needs to eat good foods on a regular basis to be healthy. Moms in particular can put feeding everyone else ahead of themselves. Moms are not always good at taking time to eat properly. If you do this often, your health will suffer. Please take time to sit and enjoy eating your meals as often as possible. I love the days when I can sit down and eat all three meals with my family. I don't leave the house without a water bottle and protein bar in my bag when I go out to do my errands. I do my best to avoid the temptation of eating fast food when I am out of the house. My waist line and my budget thank me for this.

Spiritual

After spending more than a year of being at the beck and call of aging and dying parents, I found that I was drained spiritually. Because their end-of-life care was so intense and lasted over the course of several months, my church attendance, prayer life, and devotional time all had dry spells. When I was in church, I was such an emotional mess that I spent much of the service crying. I had to release so much emotion that it was difficult to take in the spiritual refreshing that I desperately needed. My daily Bible reading and prayer time were often interrupted with calls to help with the physical needs of others. I had the most available free time of the family members, so I was called often for help. At one point, I had to ask for them to call other family members because I was so drained physically and emotionally. I was a classic example of someone in the sandwich generation. I was in the middle of caring for young children and elderly family at the same time. I was dying to self continually, and I was also not doing what I should do to keep myself healthy. I was the cream in the middle of an cream-filled cookie. I was squished between the needs of the elderly and the needs of young children at the same time. It is a draining place to be. If you find yourself there, get a support system. You need someone to lean on during the hard times.

Rest

Most people need a solid eight to nine hours of sleep each night. The needs of someone who is dependent on you for everything is easy to put ahead of self needs. I really encourage you to find respite help if your spouse is unable to help you. Talk to your husband about helping you find time to take care of yourself. This might mean a nap, time to exercise, time for a Bible study, or just time to sit quietly. If your husband has a difficult work schedule or travels a lot, find another young mom or a grandparent who can lend a hand. The years when I had four little ones under the age of eight were hard years for me to take care of myself and get enough rest.

You have to learn to FLY (Finally Loving Yourself) and take care of you. To love others and take care of them, you have to take care of your physical and spiritual health first. You are also modeling healthy living by taking care of yourself. The goal is to raise children to be healthy, productive adults. They need your good example to show them.

After reading through these strategies, I hope you are encouraged to find some ways to re-charge your batteries. Having a schedule helps me keep from running on empty. If I don't have a schedule, I tend to just work and work and work and work. When I have a schedule, I am able to put in downtimes to rest and rejuvenate. Having a schedule also shows me how much of my time is committed, and I am able to say no to people when they ask me to do something.

If you do not have a schedule, I encourage you to work on one. I will talk about schedules in a later chapter. If you are living in a house that is cluttered and chaotic, it is going to be really hard to relax. When you try to relax, you will see a hundred things you should be doing. Then guilt starts to set in. You want to avoid that, so start simple with the Baby Steps. As you establish routines, you can include your children. If you make it fun, they will see it as a good way to get necessary things done, so they can have some fun and downtime, too. Don't be a slave to the never-ending list of things to do. Start purging and decluttering. If you have less stuff around you, you have less stuff to try to maintain. Simple is a good thing. Working in 15-minute increments is a good thing, too. You will have light at the end of the tunnel of the To-Do List. You will find freedom from guilt that you aren't able to keep up with everything.

To keep from running on empty, you are going to have to love yourself enough to make changes. If you are reading this through tears because you have gone too long running on empty, start today to take care of yourself. You cannot properly take care of others if you are not taking care of yourself. Find ways to re-fill your tank and don't run on empty any more.

LOVE YOURSELF

TAKE CARE OF
YOUR
BODY AND SPIRIT

Chapter 6

Goal Setting and Organizing

Getting organized can mean something different to each of us, and it can be different depending on the season of life you are in. Maintaining organization is a mindset that hinges on the commitment you are ready to make to an organized home and homeschool.

In this chapter, I will talk about both goal setting and organizing your homeschool and your home.

Is your home a place of sanctuary?

Can it be a place of sanctuary if it is not organized?

Are you more peaceful if things are tidy and in their place?

Do you feel scattered if things are cluttered and out of place?

These questions are to help you think about your home and how you want your family to feel when they are at home. I want my home and homeschool to be a sanctuary from the chaos of the world. I have to be intentional about being organized for that to happen. What works for me in my home might not work for you. Take my ideas as a spring board for your home.

What do you picture in your mind when you think of a sanctuary?

Look around your house. Do you have stuff piled everywhere? Are you drowning in clutter? You don't have to live with clutter. Your family does not have to live in clutter. It won't be easy, but you can get rid of the clutter. You will do it one thing at a time—15 minutes at a time.

One thing I found when I started homeschooling was that it was very easy to get overwhelmed with paper, books, and other school materials. I had to stay on top of the paper that came into my house, and, with homeschooling, I also had to keep control of our school books and school papers. I am much happier and more peaceful when my house is not cluttered with stuff. My family is calmer when the house is not cluttered, and I can tell they are more peaceful, too.

What is my secret to taming the clutter? The FlyLady has taught me a lot about keeping the clutter down in my home. I want to share some of the tips I learned from her, but you will have to decide how to handle your school papers. Some states have much stricter laws about the paperwork you have to keep on file as a homeschool family. I live in a state where the laws do not require me to keep a lot of paperwork in my permanent file. I only have to keep attendance records for each student, a copy of each student's yearly standardized test scores, and a copy of their immunizations in my permanent file. Keep that in mind as I am writing about what I keep of my children's schoolwork.

Homeschoolers tend to gather a lot of clutter. It will likely be a daily job for you to thin out the clutter in your home. If you take just fifteen minutes a day to declutter, sort papers, and recycle or shred papers, you will find that you are not living with a mountain of papers and stuff on every available surface. You only need to keep the paperwork your state requires. You do not have to keep every single paper your student produces. You do not have to keep every project your children make for their school work. You do not have to keep all of their artwork. You can ask them which things they want to keep as mementos, and then you can share some of their projects with grandparents or other loved ones. Each year, have your child pick the most favorite things to keep in one box, and don't get a new storage box each year. Keep it thinned down. If there are mementos you cannot bear to part with, try to maintain these to one storage bin for a whole childhood. I saved one plastic tub of school papers and projects for my daughter. When she moved out last year, she did not want to take it with her. She left it for me. Oh, the irony of saving those projects was not lost on me. I did not save as many projects from the boys. I did take a lot of pictures. They are mostly digital pictures (clutter-free), but I have printed out some of them and made scrapbook pages for them. Take pictures of the finished projects and share these projects with others. Grandparents are a good recipient for school projects. Favorite aunts and uncles are also good candidates to receive these projects. I have saved projects over the course of a school year and entered them in the arts or crafts category at the local fair in the fall.

If you have to keep extensive records for your state, you may need a storage bin per child each year. Be sure you know how long you have to hold onto these records. You should not be asked for elementary records when your child applies to college. If you need help knowing what to log and keep for a high school transcript, there are free and paid services online to help you with that. I have some resources for high school transcripts in a separate planning e-book.

Let's talk about other paper clutter besides your children's school papers. Everyone gets a lot of junk mail every day. Have a routine to shred mail as soon as you bring the mail from the mailbox. Some people shred junk mail in the garage before it ever makes it into the house. Some people keep a shredder near their workspace at home. I keep a shredder near my kitchen trash can. I file bills as they arrive, and I shred junk mail as soon as I can each day. I also have a home business, so I have to keep paperwork for my tax return each year. I have a filing system for these receipts and necessary paperwork. I do my bookkeeping for the business each month, and I shred papers that I do not need. Follow Internal Revenue Service guidelines on retaining tax files. Do not keep every single tax return and supporting documentation for twenty or thirty years. Invest in a good shredder and thin down your paper clutter. I have nicknamed one day of the week "junk mail" day because there is one day a week that the junk mail seems to come in bulk. I don't let junk mail sit on my counter or in my "in box." I have a specific file for bills when they come in the mail. I have not gone completely paperless on my bills because I have a home-based business, and I have to have hard copies of billing statements. I do use online bill pay and online banking. I do not subscribe to a lot of magazines, so that helps with the amount of mail I have to sort through. Get a good shredder and keep it handy. Your mail should earn its way into the house. Don't be a slave to paper clutter that you get in the mail.

Another area of paper clutter is daily or weekly newspapers. I know we live in an age of Internet news, and many of us have moved from paper newspapers to online news. However, many of us are still using coupons, and the Sunday paper is one of the biggest newspapers of the week. Have a plan for handling your newspapers. Some of you are looking at your pile of newspapers right now. Recycle them. Donate them to an animal shelter or humane society. Local community groups often have paper drives. Look for an opportunity to bless someone with all those newspapers you are holding on to. I learned to read from my great-grandparents reading to me from the daily newspaper, and I still love sitting down to read a newspaper. There is just something about the paper and smell of ink that I love. But I do not love it enough to clutter my home.

You can also have too many printed books in your house. (Gasp!) I know I just said that to a lot of people reading this who are bibliophiles. The one with the most books does not win. I have my fair share of books and bookshelves in my house, but I also have purged and given away books over the years. Recently, I boxed up three boxes of school books that we no longer needed. I took them to a local resale bookstore. They gave me store credit, and I was able to buy some very nice reference Bibles for the boys for Christmas. This was a win, win, win for me. It did not tie me up online listing and selling and shipping the books. This project literally took me thirty minutes to box up the books. I spent more time picking out the reference Bibles than I did in packing up the books. I have also boxed up books to donate for use by tutors at the local Boys and Girls Club. You can look for opportunities to bless others with books you are not using. Some homeschool groups have used book sales in the spring. Watch for these events and take your unneeded books and sell them. The caveat is that you cannot go to the book sale and buy more than you take. I also take a box of free educational materials to my local homeschool mom's support group meeting each month. I encourage the moms to share resources with one another and give away things they don't need.

One area that always needs organization in my house is the kitchen. The kitchen is a big hot spot for clutter. We eat and cook in the kitchen. We do school in our kitchen. The main entry into our house is the kitchen. Things are regularly dumped on my kitchen table and kitchen counters, as well as piled up on the floor beside the kitchen door. I have to be intentional to put away the things I bring into the house, and I have to be intentional to teach my children to pick up behind themselves. If my kitchen is clean and clutter-free, I have a feeling of being in a place of peace and rest. I am not stressed out and running around trying to tame the CHAOS.

Help with Organizing Around the House

From a young age, I teach my children to help with household tasks and to pick up behind themselves. The youngest is assigned tasks based on ability, and the older ones are assigned the more difficult tasks. I spend time in the summer training them on new tasks for the upcoming school year. We do the tasks together to start off. I listen to their suggestions on how to do the job better or faster. I praise them as they take on new tasks. I write down a list of morning routines, before school, and after school tasks. They know their morning routine is to get up, eat breakfast, get dressed, straighten their rooms, brush their teeth, and complete their morning task list. This gives me time to do my morning routine, too. During the school year, we generally start at 9:00 a.m., so the morning routines have to be done by 9:00 a.m.

Breaking bigger things into smaller pieces is goal setting. My goal is to have a clutter-free, peaceful home. I need to map out a plan to get there.

In the summer, I try to space out my organizing projects throughout June and July. That way I am not spending large chunks of time organizing things. I organize different areas a little bit at a time according the Zone of the week.

What about other areas of planning and organization?

A big area of planning for me after planning our schoolwork is menu planning. Let's face it. A hungry family is not a happy family. As homeschool families, we eat a lot of meals at home. I calculated one time that I am responsible for more than 125 meals per week when I calculate the number of people in my house multiplied times three meals per day.

Once a week, usually on Friday night, I sit down and plan my menu for the next week. I consult my calendar and plan accordingly. I try to incorporate cultural meals from our studies when I can, and I use my slow cooker often. I cook in bulk on the weekend when time allows. There are times when I cook in bulk and freeze a portion of what I cooked to use for a later meal. This saves me time and money. When I have one of those crazy days, I can pull out something from the freezer, defrost it, and heat it up for dinner. It is cheaper and healthier than a trip out to pick up dinner. All of my children know how to cook based on their age and ability. My husband does not mind helping with the cooking either. We view meal preparation and cooking as a team project.

Online menu planners can be a big help in saving time and money. I have been using a menu planner and grocery builder from Build-A-Menu online. This has helped speed up my planning and shopping process. It also has helped me save money because I am planning and using things on hand in my pantry and freezer in addition to having a planned menu for the week. There is a monthly cost for using Build-A-Menu, but I think it is worth it in saving time for me.

Another great resource for menu planning is Leanne Ely's Saving Dinner books and website (www.SavingDinner.com). She has online services to help you with menu planning, and she has written several books to help you plan, shop, and prepare meals.

In this season of life, I am not an avid coupon user. I do most of my grocery shopping on Saturday, and I just do not have a lot of time to collect and organize coupons. By shopping on Saturday, I am able to keep my week days free from a long grocery shopping trip.

Buying in bulk can save time and money. We have purchased our beef from someone who raises beef, and half of a cow will last our family about ten months. We have also raised pigs, so I have access to grain-fed, organic pork at a good price. My husband and sons also fish and hunt, so I have a supply of wild game in my freezer as well. We raise chickens for their eggs. This is not only healthy for us; it is also good for teaching the boys responsibility in caring for animals. I compare prices and know where I can get the best prices on our staple products, such as milk, bread, and produce. I buy in bulk at Sam's

Club when the price is right. While I like to cook from scratch, I do not grind my own wheat and make my own bread from scratch. I have found that I can buy healthy, whole wheat bread at the local bread outlet for a very good price each week.

Goals for Exercise and Healthy Living:

Schedule exercise into your daily plan for yourself and your children:

- Indoors:

    o Exercise DVDs

    o Treadmills

    o Elliptical Machines

- Outdoors:

    o Biking

    o Basketball, Volleyball, Kickball

    o Swimming (seasonally)

    o Other Sports

We all need exercise for a healthy body, and it also gives us more energy to do other tasks around the house.

In closing, I want to encourage you that you can get organized and be successful to accomplish God's purpose for your life. He will equip you for what He has called you to do. Be intentional about your goals. Talk to your husband about your goals. Know your goals. Write your goals down. If you need accountability, find some like-minded friends, and share your goals with them. Plan to succeed in your goal by breaking them down into manageable steps. Do one thing at a time. Celebrate the small successes along the way to your big goals. Train your children to help you around the house. Teach them to be independent learners. Execute your plan. You took the time to decide on a goal and wrote it down. Now do it. Take it a day at a time.

Above all, when things do not go according to your plan, show mercy and grace. You might have to re-evaluate your goals. You might have to revise your goals. But know that, even when you do not know why things are not going according to your plan, they are going according to God's plan.

SETTING SMALL GOALS

WILL HELP YOU ACHIEVE

BIG DREAMS

Chapter 7

Check Your Perfectionism at the Door

Perfectionism is a trap. No one is perfect except Jesus. Why do we try to beat ourselves up for not being perfect? We are not ever going to achieve perfection in this world. All we end up doing is beating ourselves up for not being perfect. We compare ourselves to others around us that look like they have a perfect life. Guess what? They do not have a perfect life.

Social media is particularly bad for making us feel like we do not measure up to others. Remember that most people only put the "good stuff" in their lives on social media and blogs. They do not always share the "bad stuff" or failures. I try to be transparent about our successes and failures, but I always remember that I do not want to hurt my family by posting failures. I am careful about what I post about my family on social media and in my blog.

If you are a Christian and read the Bible, you will notice that everyone in the Bible, except for Jesus, had feet of clay. They were not perfect. They were like you and me. They had faults and weaknesses. Even with their faults and weaknesses, God used them in mighty ways.

> The Bible is
>
> filled with stories
>
> of *imperfect people*
>
> who made a
> difference.

No one else in the world can be harder on me than I am on myself. I have had to learn to let go of perfectionism and love myself just as I am. You can do it, too. Learning to Finally Love Yourself (FLY) is a big lesson I learned, and it is Biblical to love yourself. There are many verses that back that up.

Mark 12:30-31

"And thou shalt love the Lord thy God with all thy heart, and with all thy soul, and with all thy mind, and with all thy strength: this is the first commandment.

And the second is like, namely this, **Thou shalt love thy neighbor as thyself.** There is none other commandment greater than these."

Matthew 19:19

"Honour thy father and thy mother: and, Thou shalt love thy neighbor as thyself."

Ephesians 5:29

"For no man ever yet hated his own flesh; but nourisheth and cherisheth it, even as the Lord the church:"

You have to love yourself before you can love others. You can fake it, but you truly cannot love someone else until you love yourself. It is not selfish or self-centered to love yourself. Perfectionism has a way of distorting how you feel about yourself.

Perfectionism is a poison. It will consume you. It will cause you to either work yourself crazy or not do a thing. Both extremes are bad.

Perfectionism runs rampant in many families. I have seen it consume people I love. They are always trying to make everything fit into a nice, neat, perfect little box. Life is not meant to be lived that way in bondage. You don't have to work non-stop trying to achieve perfection. You will never get there on this side of heaven. Don't make yourself and those around you suffer while you try to attain the unattainable.

The opposite side of trying to achieve perfectionism by working all the time is being frozen by the thoughts that you will never measure up.

With this extreme, you will find yourself living in CHAOS (Can't Have Anyone Over Syndrome). You will begin to think it would be easier to move and start over than to deal with your home and the mess it is in. That is a lie. You can leave the thoughts of perfectionism behind and baby-step your way out of CHAOS.

The first step is to love yourself enough to make a change and break the chains of the bondage of perfectionism.

BREAK THE CHAINS

OF BONDAGE TO

PERFECTIONISM.

Balance

The opposite of trying to live in perfectionism is balance. Is your life balanced? How can you get it balanced?

Life is busy.

You have control on how busy your life is. If you are frantically running from thing to thing and feel like you are swimming upstream, it might be time to let some things go. It might be time to pass the baton to someone else for some of your activities. It might be time to start using the word "No" on a regular basis.

I found that the more children I had, the more people asked me to do. Whether it was church, extended family, homeschool groups, or Bible studies, people liked to ask me to do things or lead projects. I guess they thought that, if I had a lot of children, I had it all together and could do anything. Wrong!

Being wanted and in demand by others can feel good, but it can also take you away from your primary goals of caring for your husband and children. I have seen marriages fail where the wife was doing a lot of good things for others, but she was neglecting her husband and children. I have seen the regret in their eyes when they realized that the cost for being in demand and doing good things for others had a very high price. I have seen the regret lived out in the lives of their children.

So how do you decide what to keep in your schedule and what to drop?

When I have felt overloaded, I have done two things to help me decide what to let go. First, I spent time in prayer asking God what I should let go. I sought Him for direction and peace. I also talked to my husband. He is usually a pretty good barometer to measure my outside responsibilities. Many times he can see something that I can drop which I might not consider. He knows where my stresses are and what needs to go. The hard part of that is actually following through and dropping what he suggests.

As I have gotten older and my children are growing up, I still make it a point to have family time as much as possible. This includes family meals most nights and fun activities together. If our schedule is jam-packed with activities, we lose family meal times and play time as a family.

To figure out where you can drop some things from your schedule, make a list of your activities that take you out of the house. You might have daily, weekly, monthly, or even yearly commitments. Beside each item, rank it with a number from 0 to 10. Use 10 as your most important commitments, and use 0 for those commitments that bring you the most stress. If you have more commitments than you can list on one side of a piece of notebook paper, you will need to do some serious pruning.

You do not want your balance in life to be so heavily on the things outside of your family that your family suffers. You want a good balance of family time, outside time, and personal time.

After you rank your outside commitments, start pulling away from those things that you ranked at 4 or below. You will need to pass these things onto someone else. One year I was having a hard time scaling back my volunteer jobs with an outside group, so I took the year off from that group. Members of the group were forced to take on jobs that no one wanted to volunteer to do when I was a part of the group. It was a hard decision for me to take a break, but it was for my personal balance and the balance of my family. After a year away, the group was still going without me, and I rejoined the group as a member. I took on one job that I had previously done, and I lavished a lot of praise on those who were doing very well with my previous responsibilities. I know that is an extreme way to relieve myself of commitments, but for that season of my life, that was the best way to handle it.

Church is another area in which moms find themselves over-burdened and over-committed. Once you have a baby, you might find that churches often want more commitment from you in serving in the nursery and preschool ministries. Young moms need time in services and in Bible studies with other adults. Some of the older ladies with grown children should step up to mentor these young moms and offer to help in the nursery and preschool to allow these young moms time to recharge and get filled back up.

I can remember a time after I had my fourth child, that I was very dry physically, mentally, and spiritually. I am sure that it did not help that I was sleep deprived for nine months. My church attendance was nearly non-existent in the services and Bible study groups. Every time I went to church, there were not enough workers to leave my baby and my toddler in the nursery. I frequently had to stay in the nursery as a worker. Eventually, we decided as a family to prayerfully seek another church. I truly do not think God wants our service to the church and others to bring us to a point of a spiritual desert. God moved us to a different church, and I was able to find rest and refreshment.

Now that you have ranked your activities and dropped some of them from your schedule, take a piece of notebook paper. Number down the side starting with your normal wake-up time, and then list the other twenty-three hours in a day. Draw lines down the page to make a column for each day of the week. Start plugging in your sleep time first, and then start filling in your commitments. If you run out of spaces before you run out of commitments, you need to prune more things off your list. You need at least eight hours of sleep per night. Do not skimp on sleep to fit in more things to do. Leave some blank spaces on your calendar, too. You will always have appointments and unforeseen events crop up, so you need some flex time to work these into your schedule. Pick a day per week to do errands and appointments. Depending on the type of appointments you need, you might have to switch up the day of the week you do your errands. I know I got more in the habit of scheduling appointments and doing errands when I was already out and about when gas prices went up. I try to make the most of my time doing errands, which saves me both time and money.

Once you have your schedule mapped out, pray about it and see if it is workable for your mental health. If you still feel it is too jam packed, take more things off the list of outside commitments. The time you have your children at home is just a short season of your life. You can always add more outside commitments when your children are grown and have moved out of the house.

LIFE IS NOT

PINTEREST
PEFERCT

Chapter 8

Teaching Your Children Life Skills

One of my goals as a mom is to make sure my children have a well-rounded exposure to many life skills. I pray for their futures, and I pray that God will give me what I need to help prepare my children for adulthood and their life purpose.

What life skills do I think are important for both boys and girls?

- Home care and maintenance
- Yard care and outdoor maintenance
- Cooking skills indoors and outdoors
- General repairs
- Car repairs and maintenance
- Banking and bill paying
- Healthcare
- Doing things for others

Home Care and Maintenance

Home care includes the Weekly Home Blessing Hour, decluttering, zone cleaning, decorating, and general things you would do to make your home clean, attractive, and inviting. I want my home to be a place of respite for my family and visitors. I include my children in all aspects of home care and maintenance. By following The FlyLady's emails, I am able to work with my children through each zone in our house. We fix things that are broken; we tighten screws and check hinges; we check door knobs and door latches for looseness. We change the filters for our air system each month. During the zone cleaning time, we clean baseboards and move furniture to clean under it. Once a month, one of the boys will go "sofa diving" and pull out the thing that have fallen between the cushions during the month.

I keep a master list of things that need repair in my Control Journal. When we take care of a repair, we mark it off the list. Some repairs may be more immediate needs, and they may never be put on the list. But I have found it helpful to have a list that reminds me of the monthly things we check around the house. It is also encouraging to look back on the things we completed and see how much progress we have made.

Yard Care and Outdoor Maintenance

Yard care and outdoor maintenance can be done by almost any child depending on what you need done outside. We live in the country, so I even include my two- and three-year-olds in picking up sticks and trash in the yard. (One hazard of living in the country is that animals will carry trash from our neighbor's yard to our yard.) With child-size rakes and shovels, they can also help with leaf gathering in the fall.

The best part of leaf gathering is jumping in the leaves at the end. We usually wrap up a day of leaf gathering with a bonfire accompanied with hot dogs and s'mores. The children look forward to this every year. As the children get older, they can help with more regular yard work, which includes working with lawn equipment. By the time they are teenagers, my children have been able to use the weed eater, leaf blower, push mower, and riding mower with adult supervision. We walk around the yard area and outside of the house looking for things that need to be repaired. What really makes my day is when the children spot something that needs to be fixed, and then they come up with a plan to fix it. Encouraging and equipping them has really helped to keep our honey-do list of tasks down to a minimum.

Cooking Skills for Indoors and Outdoors

Raising a large family with more boys than girls has given me the opportunity to teach both sexes how to cook in my kitchen and outside. Teaching children to cook develops many skills from math skills to reading skills to following instructions. They learn quickly that proper measurement of the ingredients and following a recipe in order are necessary for a successful dish. I work alongside my children in the kitchen and gradually give them more and more responsibility. I have found that they eat a larger variety of foods by helping with menu planning and cooking. They feel a part of the process and decision making. Boys especially like to cook outside. We have done open-fire cooking with a fire pit, and we have a combination grill and smoker. The boys have learned to plan ahead to thaw meat to cook on the smoker. They also know that they are committed to a whole day of fire tending if they decide they want to use the smoker. They learn a lot of patience using a smoker to cook meat. The meat has to reach a certain internal temperature to be cooked properly and safely for eating, and I do supervise to make sure we don't get sick from under-cooked meat.

General Repairs

A part of home ownership means that there are general repairs that need to be made. I keep a running list of general repairs in my Control Journal. This can be a mix of home repairs, outdoor repairs, car repairs, bicycle repairs, or lawn equipment repairs. My boys have shown great aptitude for fixing things, and I provide them with parts and tools to learn to take things apart and fix them. One son likes to work on small engines, and he keeps our lawn mowers in good working order. Another son likes to work on bicycles, so he keeps our bikes in good working order. He has taken broken bicycles and fixed them back to working order. Another son likes to build things, so I try to supply with him age-appropriate building projects. All the years of allowing them to explore how things work and fixing things has paid off. Our oldest son is a plumber. Our second son is a landscaper. By having a list of things that need to be repaired, I can easily ask someone to fix things for me when needed.

Car Repairs and Maintenance

In the younger teen years, our children observe and learn about general car care and maintenance. This helps when they take driver's education classes and start driving. I also talk to them a lot about driving and why I make the decisions I make during driving. They learn to read gauges and listen for sounds in the engine that indicate a problem. They learn to check the oil level, change the oil, and they know how often to change the oil. They learn to rotate tires and replace flat tires. They learn to read a tire gauge to check tire pressure. We have regular times to clean out our vehicles, vacuum the floors, and wash them. If we go somewhere in my van, we take any trash or recyclables out when we get home. I teach them to read maps and plan a road trip without using a GPS device. I teach them to drive a standard shift vehicle and a vehicle with an automatic transmission.

Because I was raised by my grandfather who was a mechanic, I learned a lot about cars and routine maintenance at a very young age. This has been a skill set that has served me well as an adult. You don't have to be raised by a mechanic to have a routine maintenance check-off list for your vehicles.

Even though there are hundreds of types of vehicles, routine maintenance is necessary for all of them.

What are some things that need to be checked regularly on a vehicle?

- Oil level (know what kind of oil your vehicle uses and keep some on hand)
- Oil changed every 3,000 miles
- Tire pressure
- Window washer fluid
- Transmission fluid on automatic transmissions
- Radiator fluid level when the engine is cold
- Lights on the front, rear, and sides
- Horn
- Interior lights
- Trunk light, if you have a trunk
- Cell phone charger
- Spare tire (check for dry rot and tire pressure)
- Emergency supplies (first aid kit, jumper cables, extra water, extra oil, flashlight, road hazard flare, blanket, bungee cords, rope)

All of these are things I have taught my children from young ages. We do a lot of these check-offs together.

Part of good car maintenance is keeping it clean. As you are baby stepping your way with the FlyLady, you will find that Friday is the day you clean out your car. That is usually when I do the car maintenance check off list. I also do this same list before we go on a trip, but I do it several days before we leave in case any repairs need to be made.

Banking and Bill Paying

A big part of our adult life has to do with banking and bill paying. I have a savings account for each of my children. They are encouraged to put money in this savings account when they earn money or receive money as gifts. When they get their driver's license, I go with them to the bank to open a checking account and set up a debit card for their account. Because they are minors, I am on the account as a co-signer. Most banks have a student account that is free for them with a low amount required to open and maintain the account. By having the account with me as their safety net, I can help them make financial decisions and pay for things such as gas, food, or clothes. They learn budgeting skills with the benefit of having an adult oversee their account. When they get a job, they are responsible for paying for their gas, car insurance, and car repairs. They also buy their own clothes and pay for their cell phones. I teach them about balancing a checkbook and how to use online banking services.

We talk a lot about credit cards and the pitfalls of credit card use. Most students start getting credit card applications when they turn 18, so it is better to have these conversations when they are younger than 18.

If they want a vehicle to drive, they save money to buy it outright. My older children have thanked me for these lessons learned when they still lived at home. Both of them now live on their own and are self-supporting. They have not fallen into the credit card trap, and they know how to budget their money based on how often they are paid. If your children have a job, you will also have to introduce them to the system the Internal Revenue Service has established for filing a tax return each year.

Healthcare

As teenagers approach their eighteenth birthday, they should be aware of the information contained in their personal health care history. They should also know about certain diseases that are hereditary. After they turn eighteen, they will have to fill out their own health care questionnaires. I start helping them fill out these questionnaires when they are fifteen or sixteen, so they are aware of the types of information they will need for these forms. If they have had surgical procedures or allergies, they need to know how to document these and explain it to health care providers. I try to model a healthy lifestyle with eating, exercise, and healthy activities. So far, my older children lead healthy lives as young adults. None of my children are overweight because I do not serve a lot of junk food, and I encourage a lot of physical activity.

Doing Things for Others

Service to others is an important thing for our family. Whether we serve others through church or community activities, I encourage my children to do things for others. We have participated in 4-H community events, Meals on Wheels, fundraisers, volunteering at events with the local animal control officer helping to update rabies shots, and many other events to bless others. We also serve in our church in a variety of ways. By doing this from very young ages, my children have become empathetic and compassionate for others. Because we are around a wide variety of ages, my children know how to interact with everyone, from young children to the elderly. They look for opportunities to help others. I think having a heart to serve others helps tame the self-centered outlook many people have today.

Preschoolers and Young Children Learn Life Skills, Too.

Lots of my friends on social media and in real life are moms with young children. A common thread I see has to do with how hard it is keeping the house clean with little ones around. I try to encourage them to get their young children involved in keeping the house picked up and clean. I have six children, and when they were little, they could certainly make a mess quickly. But I learned to make it fun and involve them in picking up behind themselves. After all, if they can make the mess, they can help pick it up.

I baby-sit a two-year-old several days per week. When she is with us, we play a lot. But I have noticed that even my boys will involve her in the clean-up time with songs and encouragement. At age two, she likes to have positive reinforcement and encouragement. (Don't we all?) I see her respond to this with happiness in helping pick up her toys.

She likes to be close to me when I am doing different things around the house, and I try to give her little tasks that she can do on her own with a little assistance from me. She helps me move laundry from the washer to the dryer, and she hands me dry clothes from the dryer. She walks around and cleans with a FlyLady purple cloth. She can either have it wet or dry. If I am using a purple cloth, she wants one, too, and she mimics what she sees me doing.

We keep purple cloths in every bathroom in our house. A part of our morning routine is to swish and swipe all three bathrooms every day. We have a large family, so we use team work with our daily routines. My eight-year-old and eleven-year-old take turns doing the daily swish and swipe in our smallest bathroom. On a recent Monday morning, my eight-year-old offered to swish and swipe the master bathroom to help me out. He knew it was Weekly Home Blessing day.

His normal Weekly Home Blessing task is to use the purple rags to clean the windows on the kitchen door and clean the mirrors. He loves using the purple rags. He feels successful and confident using them. We can use the purple cloths with just plain water and no chemicals to bless our home and not expose ourselves to cleaning chemicals.

Another fun tool for young children is the feather duster. I have two feather dusters, and usually two of us dust at the same time. The feather dusters are very easy to use and maintain, and we dust during the Weekly Home Blessing Hour on Mondays. Dust clings to these feather dusters, and I do not have as much dust settle back down throughout the week. Each week of the month has a different Zone, and I use the feather duster in each Zone to get down any cobwebs from the ceiling or dust on the baseboards.

Having a positive attitude about blessing our home versus doing mundane chores has revitalized how we view the care of our home. This is something that I pray will see each of my children into adulthood as they start families of their own.

Teach your children

Life Skills

to last a lifetime

Chapter 9

Getting Through the Hard Times

We all need encouragement. Having been through some hard times in life, I want to share with you how I coped during those times. I hope reading what I have learned will help you if you have been going through some hard times.

If you are feeling overwhelmed with life and your responsibilities, remember that God will be with you. He won't desert you, especially in the hard times. He will give you what you need to get through each day. Breathe deep and take it one thing at a time. I have talked about baby steps in this book, and when you are going through tough times, you will have to take small steps to get through it.

Life is not easy. It can be very messy and may feel chaotic around you. What I want you to do is think about the things that bring you peace to help the chaotic feelings go away. Hopefully, you have your routines established, but even if you don't, you can work on small routines during the hard times. I think having basic routines helped my family cope during the hard times. When everything outside of my home feels crazy and chaotic, I love having a peaceful home to retreat to. It takes small routines to have a peaceful home. I am not a slave to keeping my home. I don't live in the bondage of chores and perfectionism. I view my routines as blessing my family. When we are in the midst of hard times, it helps to have small blessings in our lives.

Routines do not have to be complicated. I use a Control Journal to keep my routine list handy. I have lists for my morning, afternoon, and evening routines. I also have lists of routines that I do weekly and monthly. I do not spend hours a day on my routines. I also help my children develop routines. Each of them has specific routines that need to be accomplished daily, and they also help me with my routines as needed. By working from these lists, I can easily see what needs to be done, and I can fit these things in small pockets of time. Even when my life was the busiest with homeschooling, working, caring for elderly family members, and going back to college, I was able to keep my routines going because they were not complicated. When I had days where I didn't have fifteen minutes to complete a task, I would set my time for two minutes. Each of us can find two minutes in our day to accomplish routine tasks around the house.

When I am sick, the boys are able to help me with my routines. This is a huge blessing for me. I don't expect them to do my routines to be done exactly as I would do them, but I see how the boys are blessing me by helping me. I am thankful for them, and that they want to help me when I need it. The years when we added babies to the family were opportunities for everyone to pull together when I was on bed rest during my pregnancies. Because I spent time teaching and training my children to help around the house, they were able to do our regular routines and home blessings with minimal assistance from me. During these difficult times, my husband also pitched in and helped where needed. It was a blessing to me to have a family that pulled together when I needed them.

What happens if you don't share your Control Journal with your family? I can speak from personal experience here. I have routines that I enjoy doing, and I don't like to share them with others. Sounds a little selfish, but I find peace in my routines. One December, I had a tonsillectomy. The recovery was bad as they say it is for an adult following this surgery. I was not able to do any of my normal routines for more than two weeks. I learned quickly what happens when you do not share information with your family. My nighttime routine is always the same. I make sure I have a shiny sink before I go to bed. My family had no idea since they are all in bed before me. They just knew they got up in the mornings to a shiny sink and clean kitchen. I did not anticipate my needs following surgery. I thought I would be able to at least keep my sink shiny once a day.

What I found was that I was not able to do any of my normal routines for several days after surgery, nor could I talk. I would get up in the mornings, and my kitchen was not clean. My sink was not shiny. Oh my! Physically, I felt terrible, and I had to write notes and ask my family to help me. I learned to share my Control Journal with my family and let them help me when I needed it.

All of us go through difficult seasons in life. For many of us, one difficult season of life comes when we have to become caregivers for our parents. Having routines established in caring for your home will get you through these difficult times. During the season of life where I was providing care for parents or other elderly family members, I needed to find ways to take care of myself. I hope you can glean some ideas that will help you when you find yourself in a tough season of life.

You will need your routines to give you and your family a peaceful home. You will also need the help of your spouse and/or children to get through these times. We were blessed to have friends and family who also helped us when we needed it. If you have not dropped your perfectionism, you need to do it now. This is a time when you will need mercy and grace seasoned with patience. In many ways, your schedule and routines might have to bend to the needs of others. You may have to find a different day of the week to do your Weekly House Blessing. You might have to divide your tasks up throughout the week and do one task a day instead of all 7 on one day. You might have to wash bedding on a different day of the week. You might need someone to help you with getting those things done weekly. It is okay if you cannot do it all yourself. This is why you include your family. If a friend offers to help, let her. Share your routines and your Control Journal with those who have offered to help you. I know for many of you it is hard to accept help from others. Don't let pride get in your way of accepting help from family or friends.

Caregivers often end up sick themselves because they put their needs after everyone else's needs. If you are a caregiver, you will need to set aside time daily for self-care. You will need to eat a nutritious diet. You will need to sleep eight hours every night. If you skimp on food and rest, you will cause yourself harm. You need to exercise daily. If you can't get outside, you can do some exercises inside the house. I know what it is like to be the only caregiver in the home and how hard it is to take care of myself. I just made it a priority to find that time for my self-care throughout the day. This is a time when you will want to buy the good vitamins from the vitamin store and take supplements to help your body maintain good health.

When I have done elderly care, it has always been in their homes. When I am caring for someone in their home, I develop routines with them. In my home, we still keep as close to our regular routine as possible. It is not easy keeping two houses going, but knowing what day of the week we did certain routines helped all of us. I kept running grocery lists in a notebook for each house. That way I could maximize my shopping time as much as possible. I could also easily ask someone else to do the grocery shopping when needed. There are lots of changes as end-of-life care continues. Having some set things in my routines helped me stay calm and focused. If you visit health care facilities or hospice houses, you will notice that they have routines, which helps keep things more peaceful.

Because you have routines in place, you will find that, if an emergency happens, it is not the worst thing in the world if the routine is disrupted. You just pick up where you left off when things settle down. It will be comforting to get back into your routine if it does get derailed by an emergency. I remind myself that the flexible things are not as easily broken, and rigid things can break. I remind myself to be flexible during times of emergency or high stress.

Recently, our power was out for a couple of hours on a Monday morning due to an accident near our house. Monday mornings are my time to get the week going with laundry, the Weekly Home Blessing Hour, and dish washer running, but not having electricity delayed my routines that day. You know what? It was okay. This became a time to slowly start the week with the boys, and my routines were accomplished later in the day. My main goal was to make sure the boys had something to eat and water to drink that morning, and that the outdoor animals had food and water. Everything else could be put on hold until the power was back on. It gave me time to reflect on my list of blessings and gratitude.

Overcoming Obstacles

How do you stay on track when you face obstacles along life's way? We show a lot of mercy and grace to one another in our home when life's bumps come along. Mercy and grace are a big part of our faith as a Christian family, so it is a natural extension for us to live it out.

One area we focus on in our school is character training. We study the Bible and apply the principles from it. When the tough times come along, what we have learned in character training helps us through the difficulties.

A good example of working through a difficult situation happened to us ten years ago. My children were young, and I had been training them to get along with one another while I took my morning shower. I am sure some of you reading this can relate. I instructed them to not knock on the bathroom door unless it was an emergency that required medical assistance. At this time, I had five children who were 14 and under. I had no sooner got in the shower when I heard banging on the door. Our five-year-old son had jumped off the top bunk bed onto a double bed in his bedroom and cut his lip all the way through. Our fourteen-year-old daughter thought quickly, and she had gauze ready. I had to make a quick trip to the doctor's office with wet hair and clothes that were thrown on quickly. Our son needed stitches on the inside and outside of his lip, and we had to take him to a plastic surgeon. Training our daughter helped her to think quickly and get help, and she did not panic because I was in the shower.

During difficult days, I have learned to be flexible. We have done our schoolwork at different times of the day when needed. If an early morning appointment is unavoidable, we can do schoolwork in the afternoon. When we have an afternoon appointment or field trip, we get up early and get the paperwork part of our school day finished. I had a baby in late August one summer, and we did evening school for a few months when daddy was home and could help out. During the day, we worked on learning things around the house and working together to keep the house orderly and food cooked. This enabled me to get the rest I needed, and I was still able to accomplish our routines and schoolwork.

We show mercy and grace to one another on the hard days by being sensitive to one another. When someone is sick, we do what we can to help that person feel better. When someone has a surgical procedure, we take turns sitting with that person and getting him or her what is needed. It warms my heart to see my children look after one another like this. I have had surgery, and everyone pulled together to take care of me and the other needs in the household. This is a good time to practice what they have learned. It is really a heart attitude that comes from modeling the behavior as adults and teaching the children how to do various things around the house. We look at these tough times as a season of pulling together as a family.

The hardest school year we have had so far was when we provided in-home caregiving for my husband's parents. They both had life-shortening illnesses that required 24/7 in-home care. Having a basic routine in our home enabled us to go help daily as needed in the care of both of them. The family eventually had to hire nurses to help, but family members also stepped in to help with their care and to run errands for food and medication. Because I was home the most, I received a lot of phone calls for help. The children and I cheerfully responded to these calls, and they learned a lot about empathy and caring for others. They also saw their grandparents frequently and were able to work through the emotions of losing a close loved one. These are lessons they would not have learned if they had been in a traditional school setting. My husband's parents passed away within six months of one another during that school year. We spent a lot of time talking about our feelings and working through our grief as a family. Both sides of our family has been blessed with longevity. Because of this, I have been a part of care giving many times over the past ten years.

We have learned a lot about mercy and grace from real-life experiences. There are times when we did not always get things done on the TO-DO list, but we did things that were more important to our hearts. We grew closer as a family through these trials, and it is my hope that my children carry these lessons on mercy and grace with them the rest of their lives. Routines have been the foundation of having peace in my home even when everything else around me feels like it is falling apart.

LIFE IS NOT EASY.
YOU CAN GET
THROUGH
THE HARD TIMES
ONE STEP AT A TIME.

Chapter 10

Don't Live in Your Yoga Pants

Let's talk a little bit about what you are wearing around the house on a daily basis. Do you get dressed all the way to the shoes each day? Or are you wearing your comfortable clothes/yoga pants or pajamas all day? You will find yourself more productive if you get dressed all the way down to a pair of lace-up shoes each morning before your children are out of bed.

Why is it important to get dressed in clothes and put on shoes every morning when you get up?

Don't buy into the lie that you become frumpy and disheveled when you become a mom. You have control over it. You can decide every day to get dressed to lace-up shoes and put on a little make-up. You don't have to wear dirty, frumpy clothes. Being a mom is an important job. You don't have to shock your children or husband by getting dressed and fixed up once in a while for a special event. Every day is special. Treat yourself that way.

As a mother of six children, unless I am sick, I am dressed down to lace-up shoes, hair fixed, and make-up on every single day of the week. I do not wear a lot of make-up, but I do try to enhance what God has given me. I give my family my best, and that starts with how I take care of myself. I have had times where I had a baby who spit up a lot. Guess what? I had a lot of laundry during those times. I did not leave the baby in clothes that were soiled, and I did not stay in clothes that were soiled.

Every morning I get up and cook my husband's breakfast and eat with him. After he leaves for work, I go for my morning run. So I start my day off in running clothes but I do not stay in them all day. I can't. I sweat too much to stay in the same clothes. I come in after my run and take a shower. I get dressed, fix my hair, put on my make-up, and put on my lace-up shoes. I am ready for the day, whether it means being home all day with the children or going somewhere. I do not spend the day in workout clothes or pajamas. I would not be very productive, and I am not really showing my children a good example. My daily outfit is a pair of jeans and a t-shirt, depending on the season of the year. In the summer, I wear a lot of sundresses. I do not spend a lot of money on clothes for myself. I am a thrift store shopper for the most part. I look for good name-brand clothes, and I wear clothes that fit me. I don't wear baggy clothes, and I don't wear clothes a teenager would wear. I try to dress for the job of being a wife and mom, and that is a very important job for me.

You might wonder why I get dressed down to lace-up shoes every morning. When I first started staying home, I thought it was a little much for a mom of a preschooler and a baby to wear lace-up shoes all day long in the house. I was fresh from working outside of the home, and I was used to getting up and getting ready for the day. So this was not a novel idea to me. While it felt comfortable to be in my soft, stretchy workout pants and flip flops, it was just not ideal for me mentally to stay that comfortable all day. I am sure it was not a beautiful sight for my husband to come home to me in my sweat pants and t-shirt every day. I felt comfortable in my slippers or flip flops, but I found that I was more comfortable in a pair of lace-up shoes.

My children and I get dressed down to lace-up shoes every morning. One of my babies had severe reflux, so there were days when he and I went through several outfits a day, but every time he had spit up, I re-dressed both of us. (This was also the time in my life where I learned that a load or two of laundry a day kept Mount Washmore under control.) I found that I was more productive and had more energy when I was dressed to the shoes. My children were more active and played more, both inside and outside, if they were dressed to the shoes. We could also leave the house faster if we were dressed to the shoes. We did not struggle to find shoes so we could leave the house.

Being dressed to the shoes made me feel like a professional. I was ready for anything that came my way. Whether it be tasks around the house, errands, or emergencies, I was ready to roll because I was dressed and had my shoes on, and so were my children. Do you have things that just happen suddenly so that you have to leave the house quickly? That has happened to me many times. I have five boys, and it seems that boys play hard and accidents happen. It is nice to have everyone dressed and ready if a quick trip comes up during the day. It is also better to receive packages from the delivery person or mail person when one is completely dressed. I take my job as a wife and mom more seriously when I am dressed all the way down to my lace-up shoes.

Yoga pants and exercise clothes are made to be stretchy, so if you gain weight, they will stretch along with you. I also found that it is easier to track weight loss or gain when wearing regular clothes every day and not living in my yoga pants. After several months of wearing only stretchy clothes, a day rolls around, and you pull out a regular outfit and find that it fits a little more snugly than you remembered. When you wear regular clothes every day, you can feel when your clothes are getting snug on you. You will also carry yourself differently. Your head will be held a little higher. Your children will recognize this, and you will find that they treat you more respectfully. Your husband will also like it when he comes in from work, and you are dressed in real clothes. It makes my day when my husband comes home from work and tells me that I am beautiful.

Are there times when wearing pajamas all day is acceptable?

I would say a resounding YES to this. There are times when you or your children are sick, and you spend the day resting in your pajamas. This is completely acceptable. I found that, when I was on bed rest with my pregnancies or recovering from surgery, staying in my pajamas all day helped keep me from over-doing it. It also was a reminder to my family that I needed extra care and assistance. If my children are sick, I will let them rest and stay in their pajamas all day, too. This is just a physical reminder that we need to take it easy and rest and heal.

So you can see that there is a mental side to getting dressed down to your shoes every day. There are a few exceptional reasons for days when you don't get dressed down to your shoes. Just let those days be few and far between.

Why lace-up shoes?

Raise your hand if you like to be barefoot or wear flip flops around the house. Yes, that is what I thought. There are a bunch of you out there.

Now don't stop reading this, I like my flip flops as much as the next girl. There are a lot of things I cannot do in my flip flops. I can't run or change direction quickly. I can't go up and down my stairs quickly and safely in my flip flops. I can't move the animals safely from the barn when it catches on fire if I am wearing my flip flops. (Yes, that really happened to me one day.) I can't quickly remove my two-year-old from a dangerous situation if I am wearing my flip flops. All of these are things that happened in my life, and I am thankful I was wearing my lace-up shoes and not my flip flops. Just for the record, I put any kind of slip-on shoes in the same category as flip flops.

What about tracking germs and dirt around the house if you are wearing the same shoes outside and on errands and in the house? If that is a concern for you, then you need to have a pair of lace-up shoes you wear around the house. You can have a different pair you wear outside and on errands. I have a couple of levels of lace-up shoes. I have a pair that I wear for errands and shopping because they are a good walking shoe. I have a pair of very worn lace-up shoes that I have dubbed my mud or barn shoes. These are the ones I wear outdoors when it is raining. I have a nice pair of lace-up shoes that I wear around the house. I also have a good pair of running shoes. As you can see with this method, I have about four pair of lace-up shoes. I wear the newest pair in the house for a while, and as the others pair become worn out, I move them down the line when I buy a new pair of shoes. The most worn-out pair of shoes gets tossed. I run every day outside, so I am regularly going through my lace-up shoe collection.

What about the children? Do they need to wear lace-up shoes, too? Every day? In the house?

I can hear these questions in your head. Yes, your children need to get dressed down to lace-up shoes every morning if they are able to walk on their own. There is your absolution for the babies who are not walking yet. Once your children start walking, they need to wear lace-up shoes around the house too. This promotes better and safer walking for them. It will also help you get out of the house faster if you need to go somewhere. Raise your hand if you are late getting somewhere because one of the children could not find a matching pair of shoes or socks. Keep your hand up if you just decided to carry the toddler or preschooler because you could not find a matching pair of shoes and left the house anyway.

The moral of the story is that it is better to go ahead and have the shoes matched up and laid out with the rest of their clothes the night before, even if you are not planning to leave the house the next day. Things happen. Schedules change. You might need to leave the house unexpectedly. It is better to have a good Before Bed Routine in place and have everything laid out and ready to go the next morning.

Have you ever woken up in the morning with a sick child? Or had a phone call from your husband that he needs you to bring him something to work or that his car broke down on the way to work? These things happen in life. They have happened in my life more than once. By having good routines established, I was able to get myself and six children out of the house quickly when needed. Wearing lace-up shoes is an easy and healthy habit to incorporate into your life. Once you get used to it, you won't want to be in the house without your lace-up shoes on again.

GET DRESSED
DOWN TO
YOUR
LACE-UP
SHOES
EVERY DAY

Chapter 11

Mom Life

Over the past twenty-five years, I have worked outside the home and worked from home. I have seen both spectrums of taking care of my family and working. I have found challenges in both. I am sure you have challenges, too. American society tends to not support young mothers as they do in other cultures. Often after an American mom gives birth, she is on her own with the baby pretty much as soon as she is discharged from the hospital. I know there are cases where new moms have family or friends to help and support them, but if you read about how new moms are cared for in other cultures, American moms are often left to take care of themselves and their newborn baby. Many new moms think they need to do the same things they did before the baby was born. So a new juggling act is started. The new baby has needs that supersede many other responsibilities, so things get re-shuffled. You find that life has a new normal routine. What I would recommend is that expectant moms work out a very simple routine and set low expectations for what will be accomplished the first three months after a baby is born. This gives time and precedence to bonding and self-care of the new mom. If outside help is needed, the expectant mom should talk to her husband and family. By having a Control Journal and routines in place, it will be very easy to see what tasks can be reallocated.

Now that we have covered the newborn stage of motherhood, let's get on with talking about balancing motherhood and everything else you have going. Even if you do not have an income-producing job, you still work. Your schedule and life experiences are probably very different from your mother's experience, and yet many of us will mirror what we saw our mothers do during our formative years. My mother was a single mom, and she did an amazing job caring for us and our home. She was a stay-at-home mom for many years, and she eventually worked outside of the home while raising three children. My life experience has been different from hers since I have been married for more than twenty-five years and have six children. My mom did many things well, and I try to emulate those things as a mother. There are things that she did very well that I am just not as gifted in doing. That is okay. My mom had days of the week for different tasks, and I find that I follow a similar pattern. Some of that is due to following the FlyLady's methods, and some of it is just how my schedule has worked out. One major difference in what my mom's life and my own life as a mom is that I am also a homeschool mom. My brothers and I went to private and public school, but I have chosen to educate my children at home. That in itself has changed my schedule and tasks compared to my mother's schedule when I was growing up.

Before I started homeschooling and working from home, I had a really good schedule for getting tasks done around the house and getting dinner on the table each evening. When I started homeschooling, I had to re-evaluate my schedule and priorities. I had to learn to ask for help when needed. I had to learn more about patience and mercy and grace. I started training my children to clean up behind themselves and take responsibility when they made a mess. It was not my job to clean up behind them 24/7. It is not humanly possible to work and clean behind others twenty-four hours a day. With six children, it was very possible that there would be something to clean up behind them constantly, and I could not humanly keep up at that kind of pace.

The FlyLady's schedule has worked for me during the different seasons of my life, and I have used it in a way that works for my family. That means that I might not do a task at precisely the time she recommends in her system. If I am doing school with my children in the mornings or work outside the home, I might not get my Weekly Home Blessing Hour done on Monday morning. That is okay. I can still do my Weekly Home Blessing Hour on Monday night. Maybe my schedule shifts or I have a sick child. I can do the Weekly Home Blessing Hour on a different day of the week. It's not about guilt or not getting it done at a set time. It is about getting it done when it works in my weekly schedule. There was a season in my life for two-and-a-half years where I homeschooled, took a full college course load to get my bachelor's degree, and worked three to four days a week outside the home. This was a season when my family stepped up and helped me with the tasks around the house and with meal preparation. If I planned the menu and did the grocery shopping, my family could help with meal preparation. I would start dinner in the slow cooker at lunch time and go to work. When it was time for dinner, my family had food ready even though I was not at home. Meal preparation did not automatically fall on my husband's shoulders. We made it a team effort. Even with a very busy and hectic schedule, with planning, it is possible have a clean house and food on the table at meal time.

My current season of life has different components with my writing time and work time each day, but I am able to work from home. With the support of my family, we work together to keep our daily, weekly, and monthly tasks going. With everyone's help, we have home-cooked meals on the table every day, we are on track with our school schedule for the year, and the house is clean and well organized. I don't say this to brag, but I say it to encourage you that you can do it. It takes team work and commitment, but it is possible.

God will give you
what you need
to raise your
children.

Chapter 12

Building Confidence

One of my goals as a mom is to raise confident children, so they will be confident adults. Teaching them, giving them responsibility, and allowing them to make mistakes are a part of the process in building confidence. Allowing them to learn from their mistakes and have successes is crucial to developing confidence

Preschoolers and Young Children Can Help, Too.

Lots of my friends on social media are moms with young children. A common post I see from them has to do with keeping the house clean with little ones around. I try to encourage them to get their young children involved in keeping the house picked up. While children can make a mess quickly, they can learn to clean up quickly. I learned to make it fun and involve my children in picking up behind themselves. After all, if they can make the mess, they can help pick it up.

For example, I baby-sit a two-year-old several days per week. When she is with us, we play a lot. But I have noticed that even my boys will involve her in the clean-up time with songs and encouragement. At age two, she likes to have positive reinforcement and encouragement.

(Don't we all?) I see her respond to this with happiness in helping pick up her toys.

She likes to be close to me when I am doing different things around the house, and I try to give her little tasks that she can do on her own with a little supervision. She helps me move laundry from the washer to the dryer, and she hands me dry clothes from the dryer. This week she asked me if we could go outside to blow bubbles. I told her I could go outside as soon as I started the laundry. She responded that she would help with the laundry. She loves to walk around and play with a FlyLady purple cloth. If I am using a purple cloth or a feather duster, she wants one, too, and she mimics what she sees me doing.

We keep purple cloths in all three bathrooms in our house. A part of our morning routine is to swish and swipe all the bathrooms every day. We have a large family, so we use team work with our daily routines. My eight-year-old and eleven-year-old take turns doing the daily swish and swipe in our smallest bathroom. The two older boys take turns doing the swish and swipe in their bathroom, and I do the swish and swipe in the master bathroom.

My eight-year-old's normal Weekly House Blessing task is to use the purple rags to clean the windows on the kitchen door and clean the mirrors throughout the house. He loves using the purple rags. He feels successful and confident using them. He can use the purple cloths with plain water and without chemicals to bless our home and not expose himself to cleaning chemicals.

Another fun tool for young children is the feather duster. I have two feather dusters, and usually two of us dust at the same time. The feather dusters are very easy to use and maintain.. Dust clings to these feather dusters because they are made from ostrich feathers, and I do not have as much dust settle back down throughout the week. Each week of the month focuses on a different Zone, and I use the feather duster in each Zone to get down any cobwebs from the ceilings or dust on the baseboards.

Children also learn well from trying to figure out a problem, failing, trying again, and succeeding. Sometimes, they might fail more than once before they figure it out. This is such a great learning tool for them that will help them as adults. Successful people have successes, but you know what else they have? Failures. Have you read a biography about Thomas Edison or Alexander Graham Bell? Both of these men had great successes that we still use today, with electricity in our homes and the use of the telephone for our communication needs. When you read about them, you will learn that they had many failures before they succeeded. Isn't perseverance a trait you want to instill in your children?

What are some ways to help your child succeed? I am sure this question is in many of your minds. I have given my children supplies to make something and told them what I wanted the end result to be, but I did not give them step-by-step instructions. For instance, I have given them craft sticks, metal washers, and rubber bands and told them to make a catapult. I have also given them supplies to make a small lighthouse and told them to figure out how to assemble it and make it light up. With both of these projects, they had to figure out a process and try different techniques before they succeeded.

By giving them a safety net while they learned, they were not afraid of failing before succeeding. I have seen this translate into the lives of my young adult children. My oldest son is a plumber, and much of his day is spent solving problems. He is very successful because he has had the chance to learn by trial and error. He was fortunate to do his plumber's apprenticeship under a licensed plumber who is also a homeschool dad. His boss allowed him many opportunities to learn on the job through trial and error. Our daughter is a cosmetologist, and she has had many opportunities to learn and fix hair mistakes.

You can think of many ways to help your children gain confidence through failure and success. Start with small projects that won't discourage them when they fail. Support them and talk them through the failures. Don't give them the solution, but you can certainly guide them to find the solution for themselves.

Let your
children
learn by
doing things

Chapter 13

Helping Your Children Find Their Joy

Adulthood lasts so much longer than childhood. As you are raising your children, you want to help them find their strengths and the things that bring them joy in life. So many adults go through their entire life not doing anything that makes them happy. They exist from day to day doing mundane jobs for a paycheck. Don't you want more than that for your children?

Even very young children can show you what makes them happy in their daily play. Observe your children at play. Provide materials for them to extend their play. Understand that their interests may change over time, but as you observe and talk to them, you will always have a pulse on their interests. You can provide opportunities for them to explore more about the things that they like.

Some children love to take things apart and figure out how they work. Some children love different types of art and are very creative. Some children enjoy studying and learning intricate details about the world around them. Some children enjoy reading and writing. No matter what your children love, you can help them extend this love as they grow up.

My oldest child has a love for everything art. From a young age, art was her favorite thing to do. She loved crafts, painting, drawing, etc. I once asked her what her best school day ever would be. She told me that her best school day would be one where the only subject all day was art. I always kept her supplied with art supplies. I signed her up for painting classes. I encouraged her participation in 4-H activities. I knew her gifts were artistic in nature. She was not a strong math student. That makes sense since math and art originate from different sides of the brain. When it was time for her to consider college, she picked a program that did not focus on math but focused instead on her artsy side. She decided to go to cosmetology school. She excelled in her classes and graduated at the top of her class. She has been working as a licensed cosmetologist for four years, and she is very happy with her career choice.

My oldest son has always been a math person and loves taking things apart. I provided him lots of opportunities to figure out how things work by letting him take things apart. As he grew, he also learned to put things back to together after he took them apart. He learned to fix lots of things for me. By the time he was ten-years-old, he knew he wanted to be a plumber. I have no idea where that thought came from, but it was something that was inside of him. When he was in high school, the opportunity came for him to become a plumber's apprentice. He jumped at the chance to learn this trade, and we worked his school schedule around his apprenticeship hours. He has completed his two-year apprenticeship and will take his plumber's license exam this spring. He loves his choice of career, and he is happy and joyful in his life.

My next son is a young teenager, and he loves everything to do with the outdoors. I have encouraged his love of the outdoors by providing lots of activities outside, such as hunting and fishing. He also loves growing things and working in the yard, so he has done some apprenticeship hours with a landscaper. He might not want to be a landscaper as an adult, but this has proven to be a good way for him to see what is involved in the profession, and he is able to be outside doing this job, too.

My fourth-born child is a young teenager as well. He loves fixing things, and he has proven to be quite good at taking things apart and fixing them. He is also a very creative chef. He loves to make up recipes and create new dishes for us to eat. With a large family, this is a very much appreciated gift we all enjoy. He and I spend a lot of time talking and planning menus. He will even grocery shop with me to help pick out ingredients for his creations. In the late spring, he likes to help plant a garden and uses the fruits of his labors later in the summer. He has worked on our push mowers and fixed them when they did not work. He has a lot of talents and interests, and I will continue working with him to find that one thing (or more than one thing) that makes him happy to do.

There are still two more little boys in my house, and I work every day with them to find what brings them joy. For now, they have lots of interests, and I provide opportunities for them to learn more about those interests.

Developing my children's interests is important to me because I have met adults who have jobs they hate. They lack joy in doing something that takes up most of their awake time each day. Their unhappiness likely spills over to their home life. If you want to help your child find what interests them, get involved with different activities. We found that 4-H was a great way for our children to learn about different topics. We provided music lessons and art lessons as the children showed interest in the arts. We provided hands-on activities, so the children could figure out how to take things apart and put them back together again.

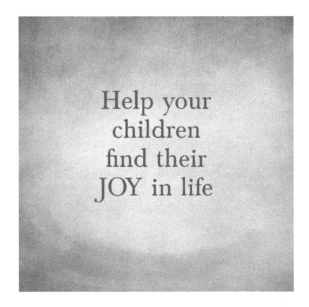

Help your
children
find their
JOY in life

Chapter 14

Letting Them Go: Giving Your Children Wings

The ultimate goal for raising my children is to give them wings so they will find their joy and can fly the rest of the days of their lives. Loving them, training them, and walking alongside them are ways to help them find their wings and soar. I don't want them to settle for mediocrity or second best. I want them to achieve their dreams and find their passions. How does having a shiny sink or decluttering help find their dreams? It removes the extra stuff from their lives, so they are not distracted with stuff and can find their purpose and passions. Living with physical clutter will lead to mental clutter. I don't want my children to grow into adults who are in bondage to physical or mental clutter.

You won't be able to do everything at one time. Set small goals and take baby steps. Reward yourself for your successes. When you work hard, reward yourself with something you enjoy doing. My children and I work hard, and we play hard when the work is done. Give up your perfectionism. Perfectionism is a trap that we can fall into easily.

Perfectionism will hold you back. Start where you are and decide that you are worth it. Your family is worth it. Let go of the guilt that you are not perfect. Don't let your children lose their mom to perfectionism.

Let me say that one more time. You need to hear this.

Let go of the guilt that you are not perfect.

Guilt will hold you back. Start with Finally Loving Yourself (FLY). You have to love yourself first and take care of yourself before you can take care of others. If you have ever flown in an airplane, you have heard the safety talk. In the event of an emergency, you are supposed to put your own oxygen mask on first and then help others. If you do not take care of yourself physically, mentally, emotionally, and spiritually, you will not be able to take care of your family.

In times of stress, the power of 15 minutes will get you through the tough times. Your children will get through the stressful times better if they know there is a basic routine to fall back on. The seasons of life are not always easy. There are mountains to climb, and there are valleys to walk through. A basic routine will see you through all of these seasons.

Learn to say "No." You will be asked to do things for others all the time. Filter these requests carefully. Pray about them. Ask your husband for his thoughts on the requests. Don't let guilt be a part of your answer. You have twenty-four hours in a day. That is only 1,400 minutes in a day. Choose how to use those minutes wisely. When you say "Yes" to something, you will have to give up something else you are already doing. Saying "No" can save your sanity, your health, and your family. Remember what is important to you. Being a stressed-out wife and mom is not a good thing for anyone. There is freedom in saying "No." Use it often when you are asked to do something by others, if it is going to cause you more stress.

Another life lesson I have learned after working online for the past nine years is to not let the computer rule your life. You can close the computer or turn it off and walk away and enjoy your family. By getting away from the computer, you will become more productive when you do need to work at the computer. As technology has grown, this can also include your smartphone. My smartphone is as powerful as my laptop, and it is probably a bigger pull to check email or social media constantly. It can be put away, too. Focus on those around you. Give your family your time and attention. Don't allow yourself to get sucked into a technological vortex. You should use a timer to help keep you accountable on how much time you spend on the computer. The internet can be a big time killer. Don't let it take over your life. If you have a smartphone, the same rules apply. You can function without constantly checking emails, texts, and social media. Your time is a gift. Don't squander it on electronics. Be present in the lives of your children.

Get out of your comfort zone. Make goals for yourself and for your family. Have long-term goals and smaller short-term goals. Make them attainable goals. Let your children see you set goals and achieve them. Include your children in your goals. Goals can be anything you want them to be. Don't be shy. Set some goals and succeed. I have set some lofty goals and reached them. If you would have told me two years ago that I would run a marathon and finish it, I would have not believed you. It took lots of small steps to build up to that distance. This philosophy can be applied to any goal. You reach your goals one step at a time.

Two of my children are young adults and no longer live at home. They have jobs. They have their own homes. They pay their bills. They have found what they love to do in life. They follow the Lord. What more could I ask for? I have spent the time with them teaching and training, and now they have their wings and are flying on their own. It was very emotional for me when they moved out. But I have found that I still have deep relationships with both of them. They both call and text me regularly. When they have a problem, they call me to talk it out. I love watching them succeed in life. This is the best season of life to experience. I am thankful I still have four more children at home that I can help in their journey to find their joy and purpose in life.

Give your children
wings, so they
can FLY

Chapter 15

Life after Homeschooling and Final Thoughts

What do you do when you are through homeschooling?

Not a lot has been written on this topic in homeschool circles. I am still a few years away from graduating my youngest child, but I still think I have something to offer on this topic after talking to several homeschool moms who have graduated all of their children.

During the homeschool years you get so caught up in life with school, home, church, family, and other stuff that you sometimes stop having your own hobbies. Being a homeschool mom should not be your hobby. If you don't have a hobby, you need to experiment and find one or more. Think back to life before you became a homeschool mom. I enjoy reading, writing, sewing, running, and biking. Some of these are things I do alone. Some of them I do with my family. Your hobby does not have to be something you do alone, but it really needs to be something that is separate from your homeschool life.

A few years ago, I went back to school and completed my bachelor's degree. I was still homeschooling five children at the time, and it seemed like my life was either homeschooling or doing college homework for two and a half years. But it was such a good time of growth for me. I learned a lot about myself and my ability to learn new things. I also worked part-time outside of the home because we had financial needs beyond my husband's salary. I made it a priority to do some enjoyable things with my family during that time because I worked very hard.

Are you saying to yourself that you don't have the time or money for a hobby? Please stop those negative thoughts. A hobby does not have to be expensive. You need to enjoy yourself and not push yourself to work and be productive all the time. I have learned that it was important to pamper myself. I think this will pay off after I am through with our homeschool journey. I will not be a worn out mom or wife. I will be a happy mom and wife who knows how to relax and have fun. I don't want to be all work and no play. That is not a good thing now while I still have children at home, and it is not a good thing for me once the children are grown up and have moved out.

There are things that I want to do when I am through with our homeschool years. I want to travel. I want to participate in ladies' Bible studies during the week. I want to be able to have lunch with girlfriends. I want to be able to serve others by volunteering in some capacity. I want to be able to enjoy playing with my grandchildren. I have lots of things I want to do when my season of life changes from being a homeschool mom. Being a homeschool mom does not define me or limit me. It is just another part of me. I want to nourish the other parts of me while I am still in the trenches of teaching my children.

Throughout this book my goal has been to encourage you no matter where you are in life. I have shared my struggles and successes. It was hard to journey back through the struggles, but if it helps one person to know she is not alone, then it was worth the journey back through the pain of the memories.

When it comes down to it, getting through the seasons of life is hard, but it is possible with God and a good support system. I know that I could not have survived the hard times without God and my support system. There were days when I could not hold myself up; it was the prayers of others that held me up. There were times when I thought I was all alone, but I was never alone. God was and is always there with me. I just have to be sensitive to His Spirit.

When I have been blessed to walk through the valley of death and see loved ones pass from this life, I am reminded to be thankful for each and every day—no matter what the day brings. There are blessings to find in every circumstance. Remember that without the rain and clouds, there would be no rainbow when the sun comes back out and shines.

Each day when you get up, think of how you can be a positive influence for someone else. This helps you start the day in a positive way. We are our own worst enemies on beating ourselves up, so think of others and how you can do something for someone else. Then think of something you can do for yourself. By taking care of yourself and doing something for someone else, you will have something to look forward to each day when you get up.

Raising my children has been the best six blessings of my life. Even the tough times have brought blessings. Watching my two oldest children as young adults is a blessing. Continuing to raise four more children is a blessing. Each new day is full of new mercies, new grace, and new experiences. Each day we learn and grow together. I pray for them daily. I pray for the present, and I pray especially for their future. I pray that I am the mom they need me to be. I pray that I give them what they need. I pray that God fills in the holes that I cannot fill.

As I am writing this final chapter, my oldest child has moved four hours away from home. I have tears of joy in my eyes as I think back on her life. It's time for her to reach for the stars and live out her dreams. I want her to soar into the future that God has for her. I want her to use her wings and FLY!

Raise your children and give them wings to fly! That is my final prayer for you and your children.

YOUR CHILDREN WILL BE READY TO SOAR INTO LIFE BEFORE YOU KNOW IT

Appendix A

Car Maintenance

Oil level (know what kind of oil your vehicle uses and keep some on hand)

Oil changed every 3,000 miles

Tire pressure

Window washer fluid

Transmission fluid on automatic transmissions

Radiator fluid level when the engine is cold

Lights on the front, rear, and sides

Horn

Interior lights

Trunk light, if you have a trunk

Cell phone charger

Spare tire (check for dry rot and tire pressure)

Emergency supplies (first aid kit, jumper cables, extra water, extra oil, flashlight, road hazard flare, blanket, bungee cords, rope)

Wash and vacuum vehicles

Home Care

Weekly Home Blessing Hour

Decluttering

Zone cleaning

Decorating

Monthly habits

Keep list of things that need to be repaired

> Change lightbulbs

> Tighten screws (cabinets, drawers, door hinges, door knobs)

> Change air filters for cooling/heating system

> Change batteries in smoke detectors and clocks

Check for expired medications monthly

Appendix C

Yard and Outdoor Maintenance

Yard and outdoor maintenance will vary depending on the season and where you live. This is just a list of ideas to get you started.

Pick up sticks (any age)

Trim yard (older teens with weed eater or push mower)

Mow yard (older teens on riding mower or push mower)

Rake leaves (seasonal; any age)

Shovel snow (seasonal; elementary age children and up)

Clean gutters (season; with parent help)

Work in flower beds (any age with adult)

Plant garden (any age with adult)

Put mulch around trees/shrubs/flower beds (any age with adult)

Clean front porch/patio/deck (any age with adult assistance as needed)

Wash vehicles (any age with adult assistance)

Cooking Skills

Moms should not be the only one preparing meals. Teach your children skills in the kitchen that will benefit the family now and will carry with them for the rest of their lives. Here's a quick check-off of skills they need to learn for cooking. Refer to your young men as chefs when they are cooking with you.

Weekly menu planning

Weekly grocery shopping

Using coupons and shopping sales

How to follow a recipe

Baking skills

Outdoor cooking skills

Packing healthy meals on the go

Appendix E

General Repairs

Small repairs around the home

Minor remodeling projects (especially tearing things out)

Painting

Outdoor repairs

Bike and toy Repairs

Lawn equipment repairs

Banking and Bill Paying

Creating a budget

Paying taxes and completing a tax return

Opening a bank account (checking and savings)

Getting a debit card

Learn about the pitfalls of credit cards and loans

Learn how to use online bill pay

Buying a car

Car insurance, tags, and taxes

Car repair budget

Gas budget

Other budget items and saving for college

Income – Getting a Job

Job applications

Work permits when needed

Appendix G

Healthcare

Once your child is age 16, you should include them in filling out medical paperwork. Here is a list of information they should know by the time they are 18.

Personal Health Information

      Drug allergies

      Surgeries

      Hospitalizations

      Medications

      Family health history

      Current physicians and specialists

      Health insurance information

Fit Lifestyle

      Exercise

      Healthy meal planning

Transcripts, College Applications, and Apprenticeships

Document your child's high school career in a transcript

Subjects and grades

Electives

Books read list

Community service projects

Look for online resources to help you prepare your child's transcript. Start in their freshman year of high school. Do not wait until their senior year.

Gear your child's high school courses for their goals and passions. Start the application process in the spring of your child's junior year. Schedule SAT and ACT testing as needed. Check deadlines for college applications. Prepare your child for the essay portion of the application process. Look at financial planning and scholarship opportunities with your high school student.

Apprenticeships in high school can count for high school credit and prepare your child for the workplace after high school.

Appendix I

Sample Daily Schedule

This is a very loose schedule. I aim for hitting close to the times listed here, but I am not a slave to the schedule or clock. If we need extra instructional time, we take it. That is the beauty of homeschooling. You move at your own pace.

6:00 a.m. – Mom gets up and starts Morning Routine

>   Breakfast

>   Quiet time

>   Exercise

>   Shower

8:00 a.m. – Boys get up and start Morning Routine

>   Breakfast (They fix their own based on what I have on hand.)

>   Morning tasks

9:00 a.m. – Start school time (*detailed on next page)

12:00 p.m. – Lunch (We prepare lunch together. We have leftovers or simple foods that are on hand.)

1:00 p.m. – Independent projects or outdoor time for the boys and writing time for Mom

2:00 p.m. – Laundry/Afternoon routines/Reading time

3:00 p.m. – Dinner prep (includes mom and boys)

Finish entrée (usually started earlier in the day in the crock pot or oven or stove top)

Chop veggies

Set table

4:00 p.m. – Daddy gets home from work.

Serve dinner

5:00 p.m. – Evening routine

6:00–9:00 p.m. – Free time/Family time

9:00 p.m. – Bedtime for Boys

10:00 p.m. – Bedtime for Parents

Appendix J

Sample School Schedule

Elementary Ages

8:00 a.m. – Morning routine

9:00 a.m. – Math

10:00 a.m. – Hands-on science and history

11:00 a.m. – Language arts

12:00 p.m. – Lunch (Great learning time for kitchen skills and talking about the morning's lessons)

1:00–3:00 p.m. – Time for independent work on projects; outdoor play; reading; afternoon routines

Middle and High School

8:00 a.m. – Morning routine

9:00 a.m. – Math

10:00 a.m. – History

11:00 a.m. – Science

12:00 p.m. – Lunch (Great learning time for kitchen skills and talking about the morning's lessons)

1:00 p.m. – Language Arts

2:00 p.m. – Afternoon routine

3:00 p.m. – Free time

* Bible time is incorporated in history and science. Electives are worked into the high school schedule according to his interest.

Appendix K

Sample Menu Plan

Breakfast

    Cereal and milk

    Eggs and bacon

    Waffles

    Muffins

    Fruit

    Yogurt

    Oatmeal

Lunch

    Leftovers

    Sandwiches

    Quesadillas

    Fruit and Cheese

    Salad or Fresh Veggies

Dinner

Meatloaf

Baked chicken (or slow cooker)

Pasta and veggies

Soup and sandwiches

Beef or pork roast

Cubed steak and gravy

Hamburgers or hot dogs

Turkey

Fish

Stir fry

Quiche

Chef salad

Tacos

Baked potato bar

Homemade pizza

Eggs and bacon (or sausage)

Pancakes

Appendix L

The FlyLady's Weekly Home Blessings

Each task takes 10 minutes or less

1) Dust

2) Mop

3) Get rid of magazines

4) Change sheets

5) Empty trash

6) Windows

7) Vacuum

www.FlyLady.net

The FlyLady's Monthly Habits

January – Shining your sink

February – Decluttering for 15 minutes a day

March – Getting dressed to the shoes

April – Making your bed

May – Moving

June – Drinking water

July – Swish and swipe

August – Laundry

September – Before bed routine

October – Paper clutter

November – Menu planning

December – Pampering

www.FlyLady.net

Appendix N

Zone Cleaning with The FlyLady

Zone 1 (Week 1 of the Month)

The Entrance, Front Porch, and Dining Room

Zone 2 (Week 2 of the Month)

Kitchen

Zone 3 (Week 3 of the Month)

The Bathroom and One Extra Room

Extra Bedroom

Children's Bathroom

Children's Bedrooms

Office

Laundry Room

Zone 4 (Week 4 of the Month)

Master Bedroom

Zone 5 (Week 5 of Certain Months)

The Living Room

Family Room or Den

Daily Routines

Morning Routine

   Get Dressed and Fix Your Hair and Face

   Swish and Swipe Your Bathroom

   Make Your Bed

   Check Your Calendar

   Start Your Laundry

   What's for Dinner

Afternoon Routine

   Eat Lunch

   Clear off a Hot Spot

   Reboot Your Laundry

   Declutter for 15 Minutes

   Drink Your Water

   Exercise for 15 minutes

Before Bed Routine

Check Your Calendar for Tomorrow

Shine Your Sink

Pick out Clothes for Tomorrow

Set Items on Your Launch Pad

Wash Your Face/Brush Teeth

Go to Bed at a Decent Hour

www.FlyLady.net

About the Author

Photo: Shane Greene Photography

Tami lives in rural North Carolina with her husband of more than twenty-five years and their children. She has been a home educator since 2000. She has a Bachelor of Science degree in Health Information Systems and uses her education to be a better teacher for her children. Tami is a writer and speaker to encourage moms. She writes reviews and other details about her life with her family at www.TamiFox.net. She is in the trenches just like you and takes life one step at a time with mercy and grace. You can contact Tami through her blog or through email at Tami@TamiFox.com.

LIKE Tami's page on Facebook: https://www.facebook.com/tamikfox

FOLLOW Tami on Twitter: https://twitter.com/tami_fox

FOLLOW Tami on Instagram: https://instagram.com/tami_fox/